SILENCE IN HENRY JAMES
The Heritage of Symbolism and Decadence

SILENCE IN HENRY JAMES
The Heritage of Symbolism and Decadence

JOHN AUCHARD

The Pennsylvania State University Press
University Park and London

Excerpt from "Burnt Norton" in *Four Quartets*, and "Ash Wednesday" in *Collected Poems, 1909–1962*, both by T. S. Eliot, copyright 1936 by Harcourt Brace Jovanovich, Inc.; copyright 1943, 1963, 1964 by T. S. Eliot; renewed 1971 by Esme Valerie Eliot. Reprinted by permission of the publisher.

Library of Congress Cataloging-in-Publication Data

Auchard, John.
    Silence in Henry James.

    Includes bibliography and index.
    1. James, Henry, 1843–1916—Criticism and
interpretation.   2. Silence in literature.
3. Nothingness in literature.   4. Negation (Logic)
in literature.   5. Symbolism in literature.
6. Decadence in literature.   I. Title.
PS2127.S54A93 1986   813'.4   85-21750
ISBN 0-271-00420-7

To my parents
John Thomas Auchard and Elinor Sanches Auchard

Contents

Acknowledgments

I would like to express sincere appreciation for a summer grant awarded me in 1982 by the General Research Board of the University of Maryland. But I am particularly grateful to my colleagues in the English Department; under the chairmanship of Annabel Patterson the senior faculty moved to give new assistant professors a semester's leave time early in their careers. The help was enormous.

Lewis Leary recognized the importance of silence in Henry James before I did, and he told me about it. It is largely because of him that this project got under way and finally was completed. And so in one more way I owe him a debt of gratitude. But I would be heartless indeed if I did not record an equally important debt to Mary Warren Leary— for encouragement, warmth, and generosity. Anne Hall and Max Steele, my colleagues at the University of North Carolina, provided sure direction at the beginning of this study, as did Elizabeth Loizeaux, my colleague at Maryland, near the end. Alan Solomon of the Library of Congress gave me great assistance at various stages of my research, Bob Haliday offered a word processor and matchless interest, and Abe Nainan distinguished himself as a model of helpfulness and inhuman punctuality. Many friends deserve my gratitude for their support, but at this point let me name three—Thomas Jessiman and David Gibson, for their spirit, and Gemma Spinelli, *per il suo spirito*.

Preface

Near the turn of the century the American imagination seemed preoccupied with worldly concerns. Some observers spoke of heroic materialism, some of mammon, but most agreed that bourgeois ambition had asserted itself and that transcendental musings were, at best, part of nostalgia. But while industrial expansion accelerated, and while a good citizenry invented linotype machines and literary realism, a *fin-de-siècle* was approaching on the European continent which had little to do with the confident materialism of the New World. As prominent literary figures looked away from repugnant concerns of smiling merchants and smiling progress, they grew more and more fascinated with nuance, with refinement, and with modulation; indeed, some among them looked so far away from the pulses of ordinary life that critics caught the scent of gaminess in their work and in their subtle passions. They turned against naturalism, against realism, against positivism, against phenomena. The shadowy, crepuscular symbolist movement began to explore a consciousness more evanescent and diffuse than any psychology had yet attempted. It is the claim here that Henry James entered those shadows and thrived among them.

As the symbolists abandoned more common concerns, some among them moved into hothouse gardens, rich in discriminated delicacy, but enervating places that could foster little or no hardy growth. The supersubtle and hyperaesthetic symbolist habit sometimes allowed rarefaction all the way into the extreme of decadence, where positive pleasure became confused with negations of every kind. It may startle some to find the respectable Master linked to the decadent movement, and therefore at the outset I would state that the term "decadence" is used in this study, almost always, in a descriptive or historical sense, and not in a judgmental one. It is a term used with considerable latitude, for it must comprehend the inhuman connoisseurship of Gilbert Osmond, the imaginative perverseness of his wife, Milly Theale's sublime yet tortuously negated definition of life, as well as many other conditions. Decadence should not be understood as a pose which borders on the camp—and surely the celebrity of Oscar Wilde always raises that possibility—but rather as a serious, seductive vision of life which well might attract fine people.

Part of the heritage of symbolism and of decadence is the road back which the Church provided for some. The symbolist impulse, balanced as it was on the edge of the unworldly, at times remained shakily secular. Whether lured by the graceful ordering of aestheticized Catholicism or by the stronger vibrations of mysticism, many in the forefront of the movement returned to the Church's positivism, even if that positivism followed the extreme ascetic path of a Johannine *via negativa*. J. K. Huysmans, creator of the Duc Jean Des Esseintes, perhaps the most famous fictional decadent, eventually wrote of the dead end to which perverse over-refinement had taken him; he agreed that such a progress must lead to the muzzle of a pistol or to the foot of the Cross. Those not so strongly committed to decadence as Huysmans—or perhaps simply not so wasted by it—would remain secularists who experimented only with the dressings of the Church, picking and choosing artifacts from among the ecclesiastical trappings. James himself was more than merely aware of the progress of symbolism, of decadence, of experiments with high-church ritual and ambiguous reconciliation. His work was part of that progress.

A study of the silences in Henry James must consider such historical moments; yet it must point further. Finally, James's fascination with the anti-phenomenological universe cannot be claimed by any particular movement. The pervasive sense of negation—of ubiquitous absence, of silence both metaphoric and persistently literal—presents an idiosyncratic artistic intelligence which at times seems overwhelmed by various pulses of nothingness. Pascal spoke of the terror of infinite spaces, and indeed the terror in the later James, built up through increasingly oppressive and complex silences, moving through sometimes glimmering and sometimes darkening landscapes, seems poised on the brink of the Pascalian void. As a symbolist expression, silence in Henry James provides a delicately balanced emblem of modern man's existential ambiguities, a stopping point where either/or assertions of *plenum* and *void* meet and flicker one to the other, now voicing the claims of belief and now those of nihilism. Perhaps the West may be just on the threshold of deeply appreciating the language of silence, and many might agree with Susan Sontag that the appeals for silence are stronger today than ever before. But they have been expressive for many years.

A modern interest in silence has moved out in many directions. Even the shortest list of relevant critics would cite the contributions—sometimes rigorously systematic, often suggestive and poetic—of Sartre, George Steiner, Tzvetan Todorov, Heidegger, Merleau-Ponty, Hannah Arendt, Wittgenstein, Sontag, and John Cage. Ihab Hassan delineates at least ten different definitions of literary silence, from "a perversion of vital and erotic processes" to "alienation from reason, society, and history"[1]—while Wayne C. Anderson crisply examines it as a "rhetorical strategy of discourse" and grumbles at abuses which allow the term to "mean anything from narrative obliqueness to deconstructive absence."[2] As long as people continue to write book-length studies on wordlessness, these terms will accumulate troublesome uncertainty, along with resonance. John Cage's musical pauses must always differ from the verbal gaps of linguistic studies, which again stand apart from the "silences" Robert Goldwater sees depicted in European paintings exhibited between 1870 and 1900. None of these silences can receive treatment in isolation from the others.

By silence I primarily mean just that, the absence of talk, the holding back of words—the early refusal of Christopher Newman to expose the Bellegardes, Maggie Verver's much later refusal to tell what she knows of the affairs which threaten her family. But as a complex symbolist issue, silence, as structure, relates to other "negated" forces in the fiction, those which move against obvious statement, against presences, against things, against the assertions of positivism. Even ghosts, as visitations which live as absences, become part of the progress of Henry James away from phenomena and the word. The vacant, the void, the blank, and the dead all participate in the pressure of silence, supplying the furniture of an increasingly quiet, increasingly anti-materialistic consciousness.

I have treated in depth two novels from the early period, two from the middle years, and two from the major phase. Each paired work moves, I believe, in a direction different from that of its chronological partner, and therefore the study would suggest a persistent swing between polarities, perhaps most clearly indicated by the chapter titles on the *via negativa* and the *via positiva*. James's work often suggests the pulse of thesis and antithesis, and my selection of representative works attempts to demonstrate that dialectical process.

An Introduction suggests the context for an examination of symbolist silences. Such a context must be far-reaching, touching on poetry, the theater, orientalism, mysticism, art, music, science, and philosophy. Symbolism, a term perhaps not as furiously multitudinous in meaning as romanticism, demands both a certain focus and a range of suggestive associations. Chapter 1, a necessarily preliminary chapter, examines *Roderick Hudson* and *The American* as two immature works, important in this context because they introduce many formative structural silences which will recur in later fiction, in far more complex patterns. *Roderick Hudson* stands alone in the James canon as a work in which a character moves toward a positivity of experience that has little to do with symbolist silences and absences. The shift from the Italian capital to Paris in *The American* demonstrates a growing sense of the potential for fertility in the withdrawn and the negated. Chapter 3, on the tales, examines the insinuation of darker impulses throughout the career; it attempts to suggest the line which divides the symbolist strain from more sure decadent and egotistical extremes. The ghostly forces are here related to major thematic and structural concerns. They provide, I believe, intensified expressions of ambiguous absences, forces which appear throughout many of the mature novels.

Chapter 4 argues that Isabel Archer displays the exaggerated anti-phenomenological bias of the symbolists, and that her preoccupation draws her close to vitiating decadence. The marriage she makes indicates the risks such imaginative consciousnesses face, and it suggests the grim yet powerful appeal of subtly evolved aspects of negation. The chapter explores the developing confusion of positive and negative in James and argues that the marriage to Osmond suggests an insidious attraction to decadence. Part of the intention here is to indicate that at times antipodes of spirituality, or ecclesiasticism, and decay seem surprisingly close.

Chapter 4 also presents the dialectical opposition of *The Spoils of Poynton*. It views Fleda Vetch as a young woman with perceptual habits contrary to those of Isabel Archer. Archer emphatically may reject the lure of phenomena, but Fleda believes that "things are the sum of the world." Despite her pleasantly educated taste in the plastic arts, she begins as a thinly disguised seeker after materialism, slowly to awaken to the silences of regenerating symbolist concerns. Standing midway between the good-natured renunciations of Christopher Newman and the highly spiritualized ones of Milly Theale, Fleda Vetch suggests the link between negation and force which later heroines will develop— here unblemished by the taint of decadence.

Chapter 5 discusses *The Wings of the Dove*. It is for the reader to decide if the story of Milly Theale is decadent—or highly spiritualized— but this chapter develops the interplay of an overwhelmingly negative perceptual bias which relates to symbolism, to decadence, and to aestheticized Catholicism. Central to this examination is a sense of a *via negativa* which was associated with the "wave of mysticism" that swept through the final decades of the nineteenth century. Here I make a suggestion which I hope some readers may find fruitful. Although no sure links can be made, perhaps some evidence indicates that the intensely ironical stance of *The Wings of the Dove* may have derived force from the unyielding regime of St. John of the Cross. The negative way is presented as, in Henry James, quasi-spiritual poeticism which uses profound ironies to define negative as positive and positive as negative. The chapter argues that the novel moves to the edge of religious statement but never makes that statement.

Chapter 6, on *The Golden Bowl*, demonstrates the strong swing of the Jamesian dialectic. The novel opposes the *via negativa* and attempts to bring the supersubtle symbolist awareness back to worldly applications. Although Maggie Verver's story is as informed with silences as that of Milly Theale, the later novel lacks, almost completely, the negated spiritual sense of the earlier work. Silence, as positive psychological method rather than as spiritual evacuation, faces profound social breakdown and actively works for reorganization. The chapter posits a *via positiva*, where a developed symbolist awareness works for the pragmatist, and that pragmatist moves toward worldly success. The silences in *The Golden Bowl* help control a pervasive and growing terror, which, finally must be considered as an existential concern.

The conclusion inevitably attempts many things, but primarily it would suggest a poetic imagination so intensely aware of non-being and non-expression that it seems already haunted by the existential murmurs of the modern age. Silence in Henry James may indeed be a source of integrity, vitality, and even fertility, but it plays out its subtle dialectic on the edge of nothingness and sometimes on the brink of collapse.

Although at times the effort here will provide stylistic analysis, the study is fundamentally not one of the poetics of silence. I would make structural, historical, and thematic links in an effort both to synthesize the range of negation in James's fiction and to put that synthesis into a coherent context.

The more generally available revised text of the New York Edition tends to blur distinctions and developments throughout the chronology. Therefore the primary texts are those of the first American editions of the novels and of the "original book form" of the tales.

1 Introduction:
"The Gospel of Silence"

"He understands so much that we almost wonder he can express anything."
Henry James on Turgenev

In an 1883 review of the Carlyle-Emerson correspondence, Henry James wrote that:

> It is one of the strangest things to find such an appreciation of silence in a mind that in itself was, before all things, expressive. Carlyle's expression was never more rich than when he declared that things were immeasurable, unutterable, not to be formulated. "The gospel of silence, in thirty volumes," that was the happy epigram of one of his critics, but it does not prevent us from believing that, after all, he really loved, as it were, the inarticulate. And we believe it for this reason, that the working of his own genius must have been accompanied with an extraordinary internal uproar, sensible to himself, and from which, in a kind of agony, he was forced to appeal. With the spectacle of human things resounding and reverberating in his head, extraordinary echoes, it is not a wonder that he had an ideal of the speechless.[1]

The happy epigram—the gospel of silence, in thirty volumes—with slight modification and slightly less insistence, might describe the complexity of Henry James's own work. Over the next twenty years James himself would make a complex retreat from the word.

In James's fiction vitality often derives from the force of silences. Exceptionally powerful in the novels, over tea or over abysses, some silences are merely polite and social, others profoundly moral and philosophical. James explores how the superficially bare, quiet, and passive can signify fulness and activity, and how the seemingly engaged life can add up to an insignificant affair. Language itself becomes antilanguage, and silence—not merely dumb tribute to the incommunicability of things—becomes charged expression and the major force of human action.

Sartre was one of the first to appreciate the rumblings of a literature of silence after World War I, and he was to make the claim that Jules Renard began it all, created the literature of silence.[2] It had, however, rumbled before, with Carlyle and then with James. Speaking with a resounding emphasis that James would never attempt, in *Sartor Resartus* Carlyle wrote:

> SILENCE and SECRECY! Altars might still be raised to them (were this an altar-building time) for universal worship. Silence is the element in which great things fashion themselves together; that at length they may emerge, full-formed and majestic, into the daylight of life which they are thenceforth to rule. . . . Speech is too often not, as the Frenchman defined it, the art of concealing Thought; but of quite stifling and suspending Thought, so that there is none to conceal. Speech is too great, but not the greatest. As the Swiss Inscription says: *Sprechen ist silbern, Schweigen ist golden* (Speech is silvern, Silence is golden); or as I might rather express it: Speech is of Time, Silence is of Eternity.[3]

Sartre understood that the dangerous irony of the literature of silence was that "finalement, ce gout du mutism la ramene au badinage. On peut bavarder en cinq mots comme en cent lignes. Il suffit préférer la phrase aux idées" [ultimately, this taste for muteness leads to trifling. One can chatter in five words just as well as in one hundred lines. It is only necessary that you prefer expression to ideas].[4] If, perhaps, T. S. Eliot was right to claim, subtly, in praise of James, that the novelist's mind was so fine it was never violated by an idea, the unsympathetic critic might use Sartre's words as basis for attack on James. Some may claim that the prolixity of the later novels trails off into genteel but unmistakable chatter, into *badinage*. It is the intention here, however, to demonstrate the significance and power of the silences, despite all the words.

Sartre knew he was overstating. Even in the West the literature of silence began long before Renard's gnomic expressiveness. George Steiner has spoken of the "crisis of poetic means, as we now know it, [which] began in the late nineteenth century. It arose from awareness of the gap between new senses of psychological reality and old modes of rhetorical and poetic statement."[5] Steiner claims that "the circle has narrowed tremendously, for was there anything under heaven, be it science, metaphysics, art or music, of which a Shakespeare, a Donne, a Milton could not speak naturally, to which their words did not have natural access?" However silver-tongued James's characters may appear, they speak haltingly, in response to a loss of faith in language. Although they are not in the position of Büchner's Wozzeck, stuttering helplessly in the face of vicious realities, and although their speech rarely breaks audibly, it is severely limited. Despite sublime discursiveness, James demonstrates no pre-eighteenth-century confidence in the sphere of language. This is no surprise in a world which, as Steiner reminds us, the non-verbal codes of mathematics, symbolic logic, and chemical equations have moved even to the threshold of ethics and aesthetics.

There were quiet rumblings with Emerson and Carlyle, but the symbolists Mallarmé and Maeterlinck were the first seriously to attempt articulation, through silence, of beliefs and forces that had been lost to the nineteenth century. Matthiessen noted that James "did not, like Mallarmé, start with the symbol. He reached it only with the final development of his theme, and then he used it essentially in the older tradition of the poetic metaphor, to give concretion, as well as allusive and beautiful extension, to his thought."[6] Although their symbolic methods differed considerably, both Mallarmé and James worked through similar structural patterns. May Daniels has called Mallarmé's poetry that of "virtuality." She writes that, "As reality is only an imperfect indication of the rich potentiality of 'le Néant,' so the true value of the written word lies in the wealth of the suggested, unexpressed ideas contained in the symbolic blank which surrounds it. That blank, that silence, holds the real poem." Daniels goes on to quote from Mallarmé— "Tout devient suspens, disposition fragmentaire avec alternance et vis-à-vis, concourant au rythme total, lequel serait le poème tu, aux blancs; seulement traduit, en une manière, par chaque pendentif" ["Everything will be fluid, the arrangement of parts, their alternation and interruption by blank spaces, and will yield a total rhythmic movement, the silent poem, itself, translated in its own way by each unit of structure"].[7] James himself expressed similar views.

In "The Art of Fiction" he explained that the imaginative mind "takes to itself the faintest hints of life, converts the very pulses of the air into revelations." The mind catches bits of "experience," which is "a kind of huge spider web of finest silken threads suspended in the chamber of the consciousness, catching every air-borne particle in its tissue."[8] This is experience at its richest in Henry James, emptiness and void, criss-crossed by threads which catch the occasional mote, and here James makes his closest approach to Mallarmé. There is nothing here anything like the plea for saturation with the stuff of life which "Be one of the people on whom nothing is lost" superficially may imply, but rather there is the encouragement to cultivate an imagination which is an immense vaulted space, mostly quiet and mostly bare. James describes how an English novelist managed to communicate a strong impression of French Protestantism. Climbing a stair, she once glimpsed the family of a *pasteur* at supper. Her mind clicked on the scene and she continued her ascent—"The glimpse made a picture; it lasted only a moment, but that moment was an experience. She had gotten her direct personal impression, and she turned out her type." The instantaneous impression acted like an air-borne particle in the immense chamber of her consciousness, and the tension and pull of that which was unseen and unspoken worked the creation. The energy of "The Art of Fiction" derives from the essentially absent and quiet. The image of James as voyeur, ravenous for details, is false. Had the Englishwoman marched into the room with Henrietta Stackpole's determination and had she sat foursquare at the table to share a meal and a hundred meals with the family, had she demanded the real thing without gaps, silences, and absences, she might have interested James very little. The idea of James as hungry observer may be a misleading cliché. Journalists, the simplistic realists in Henry James, are generally the fools of the piece.

For years grouped among the realists, James probably stands closer to the Continental authors who had repudiated that dominant trend in nineteenth-century fiction. Recent critics have found themselves more comfortable grouping Henry James with the "new realists of Flaubert, Maupassant, Vsevolod Garshin, and Ivan Bunin," rather than the classical realists of Balzac or Zola, but some have understood James as a modernist working closer to impressionism. H. Peter Stowell in fact places James the impressionist midway "between the declarations of

realism and the manifestos of expressionism, symbolism, and imagism."[9]
It is the argument here, however, that in time James found even impressionism too limiting and insufficiently expressive, found with Odilon Redon that it had a "low vaulted ceiling," and found with Gauguin that it "neglected the mysterious centres of thought."[10]

These mysterious centers of thought or consciousness were at the heart of the symbolist intention. Robert Goldwater calls the philosophical idealism of symbolism a revolt against both positivistic scientific attitudes and the "sole concern with the world of phenomenon" which had dominated the middle years of the century. Some symbolists felt that the break from realism was not coming fast enough, and along with Arthur Symons in his 1899 Symbolist Movement in Literature, they dismissed impressionism as attempting only "to render the fugitive aspects of a world which existed only as a thing of flat spaces, and angles, and coloured movement, in which sun and shadow were the artists."[11] The symbolists pursued what James referred to in The Portrait of a Lady as "the eternal mystery of things," and they often did so through the exploration of reticence and the unspoken.

Goldwater has cited Redon's late painting "Silence" (1911) as "an epitome of symbolist style and intent."

> This figure with closed eyes and fingers to the lips, removed from the framing oval into an indeterminate space, only partially emerging from the surrounding darkness, contains the suggestion of the mysterious reality beyond appearance that is proper to symbolism. Both in its subject, which stresses a concentration upon the unseen and the unheard, and in its handling, which suggests more than it depicts, it is characteristic of the movement.[12]

Many other symbolist paintings, among them Redon's "Closed Eyes" (1890) and Lévy-Dhurmer's "Silence," embody, as Goldwater notes, the "same theme of reserve, isolation, and deeper reality, without the use of any specific iconography, thereby coming closer to the identification of subject and form which was central to theoretical ideisme."

Such themes were reiterated again and again. In 1888 Georges Rodenbach's Du Silence and La Regne du Silence provided poetic treatment of the quiet and the isolation necessary to attain to what were perceived as mysterious essences. In 1893 Maurice Beauborg's The Wordless Life was presented at Lugné-Poë's Théâtre de l'Oeuvre, and

Xavier Mellery's *The Soul of Things*, inspired by Rodenbach, worked to transform, through drawings, everyday objects into mute symbols in an attempt to get at "the occult voices of heaven," which, Goldwater states, were felt "not in conventional attributes but more directly through the rendering of the empty crepuscular space of his own familiar interior." The phrase itself is reminiscent of the immense chamber of consciousness in "The Art of Fiction." Yet there is little softness or sentimentality in the focus of such a consciousness. Writing on symbolist expression of "Maeterlinck as Mystic" Symons reiterated that "All art hates the vague; two opposites very commonly confused is the secret with the obscure, the infinite with the indefinite."[13] James worked as a subtle craftsman in his anti-phenomenological exploration, and his expression ultimately would echo Symons's 1899 manifesto.

> Here, then, in the revolt against exteriority, against rhetoric, against a materialistic tradition; in this endeavor to disengage the ultimate essence, the soul, of whatever exists and can be realised by the consciousness; in this dutiful waiting upon every symbol by which the soul of things can be made visible; literature, bowed down by so many burdens, may at last attain liberty, and heavier burden; for in speaking to us so intimately, so solemnly, as only religion had hitherto spoken to us, it becomes itself a kind of religion with all the duties and responsibilities of the sacred ritual.[14]

The creator of Milly Theale shares much with those symbolists who were preoccupied with *le néant* and *l'inexprimé*, nothingness and the inexpressible, and who led the dramatic movement variously named the *"théâtre du silence," "théâtre d'attente,"* and "static theatre." They sought for the stage the full eloquence of reticence. Among the movement's most energetic spokesmen was Maurice Maeterlinck, the Belgian dramatist whom Symons included in his groundbreaking book and whom James had read, reviewed, and, in the later novels, referred to both directly and by allusion several times. Carlyle built the "gospel of silence," but Maeterlinck was that gospel's fiery evangelist. In *The Treasure of the Humble* Maeterlinck writes:

> There is the instinct of superhuman truths within us which warn us that it is dangerous to be silent with one whom we do not wish to know, or do not love: for words may pass

between men, but let silence have had its instant of activity, and it will never efface itself; and indeed the true life, the only life that leaves a trace behind, is made up of silence alone. . . . So far I have considered *active* silence only, for there is a passive silence, which is the shadow of sleep, of death, or non-existence. It is the silence of lethargy, and even less to be dreaded than speech, so long as it slumbers; but beware lest a sudden incident awake it, for then would its brother, the great active silence, at once rear himself upon his throne.[15]

James admired Maeterlinck, but at times he himself runs the risk of too much staginess when paying tribute to the dramatist. In *The Wings of the Dove* there is:

the likeness of some dim scene in a Maeterlinck play; we have positively the image, in the delicate dusk, of the figures so associated and yet so opposed, so mutually watchful: that of the angular, pale princess, ostrich-plumed, black-robed, hung about with amulets, reminders, relics, mainly seated, mainly still, and that of the upright, restless, slow-circling lady of her court, who exchanges with her, across the black water streaked with evening gleams, fitful questions and answers. The upright lady, with thick, dark braids down her back, drawing over the grass a more embroidered train, makes the whole circuit, and makes it again, and the broken talk, brief and sparingly allusive, seems more to cover than to free their sense.[16]

Nonetheless, the pregnant symbolist silences—when narrated in Henry James—do not often strain into the histrionic, as they may have for Maeterlinck's audience. Silence can work uneasily on the stage, where the expressive actor must stiffly configure his body, often until mannerism shifts into baroque, in an attempt to suggest, in Maeterlinck's highly charged words, silence's "somber power and its perilous manifestations." Even Maeterlinck's 1894 translator and champion, Richard Hovey, admitted to the stiff puerility of much that passed before the Maeterlinckian audiences.

James may have learned from the *théâtre du silence*, although he may not have learned everything equally well. His plays were mostly failures. Perhaps one of the reasons those plays—or rather cinematic versions of his novels—now work so well, and so often, may be because the potency of silence communicates more effectively in a medium which allows intense close-up, visual flashback, and the swell of "unheard" background music. The nineteenth-century stage actor must have stood there, silently, often in a near-expressionistic pose, and the effect may have been to American audiences—unaccustomed to the severe stylization of Racine—that of caricature. In the meantime, people in the audience coughed. As John Cage has said, "There is no such thing as silence. Something is always happening that makes a sound."[17] Film may provide a happy opportunity for a glutted silence, in Sartre's term, "une silence sursaturé,"[18] for the fictive tension is far easier to maintain today. When, in a television production of The Golden Bowl, Maggie Verver wordlessly stands there, the camera might move around her, and the emptiness the view attends may fill with the insinuation of a baroque fugue. In the novel, however, James had none of the options of such techniques; he had to invent potent artistic expressions of silence, and that he did. Sontag understands that the artist "can't embrace silence literally and remain an artist; what the rhetoric of silence indicates is a determination to pursue his activity more deviously than before." Through devious structures James worked toward a correlative of that force—through absences, voids, gaps, vacancies, lacunae, and ghosts.

When Yasunari Kawabata delivered his 1968 Nobel Prize acceptance speech, he spoke at length of the major difference between the literatures of the East and those of the West. In the East the disciple of truth "departs from self and enters a realm of nothingness. This is not the nothingness or the emptiness of the West. It is rather the reverse, a universe of the spirit in which everything communicates freely with everything, transcending bounds, limitless."[19] Going on to speak of the extreme condition of "silence like thunder," Kawabata asked that the "emptiness" of his work not be taken for the "nihilism of the West." The potentialities of the silent, the absent, and the empty have been concerns of Chinese and Japanese literature for millennia. Particularly in the Tao Te Ching of Lao Tzu and the "poetry of stillness" of Li T'ai, the impulse of the reclusive, quaverless tranquility has been viewed as central to the fulfilled life. Although these concerns, as central pulses, are relatively new to the West, James upon occasion approached their essence. Yet it should also be said at the outset that, for the most part, silence in Henry James is not oriental. At times it can be Machiavellian, a subtle battle of the streets and parlors. Nonetheless, the oriental model may provide important insights.

Phenomenologist Don Idhe has indicated the most important differences between the artistic impulses of Japan and those of Europe, and in so doing he perhaps has suggested fruitful reference for this study. Speaking of the bias of the West, Idhe writes:

> Our traditional way of viewing would say that the subject matter—what stands out and is dominant in the foreground— is the sparrow or the blossoming branch. The background is merely empty or blank. . . . Yet the emptiness and openness of a Japanese painting is the subject matter of the painting, the sparrow or the branch being set there to make openness stand out. In this, there is a radical reversal: the foreground is not dominant, the background is not recessive. To understand such a painting calls for a deep reversal in noetic context.[20]

Some readers who fail to appreciate James because nothing, or at least not quite enough, "happens," may be readers overly accustomed to a tradition which concentrates on the phenomena of the foreground and fails to respond to the blankness of the recessive universe which surrounds those phenomena. If James is read with something of the noetic reversal which Idhe suggests, the modalities of silence transform into the vibrant, the rich, the thunderous, of Kawabata's terms.

Nonetheless, despite all the consideration of eloquent silences, forceful passivity, and plenitude through absence, at moments the emptiness may seem a decadent fascination and an unmistakable chill throws all into question. At such moments a John Marcher understands the quiet jungle of his life as a mute desert expanse. Absolute nihilism is impossible to communicate in literature, perhaps, as Richard Poirier has demonstrated, because the style of prose and the fluidity of language create a world elsewhere which builds its own landscape. And the density of such a landscape in Henry James might work to hide the void from our sight, as it might not with a Hemingway or a Beckett.

Cage is probably right that we never attain the condition of silence, for something always makes a sound. Sontag, speaking of "the positivity of all experience at every moment,"[21] implies the impossibility of absolute nihilism. Emptiness must by necessity remain incomprehensible, and so inevitable ironies will accrete to any void an impure richness.

We remember that the neurologically blind see nothing, not even blackness, and nothing, the perceptual psychologists tell us, is what we see with the back of our heads. True nihilism, pure silence, even as metaphor, is an impossibly unnerving concept, but the complex symbolist silences of Henry James resound with rich and varied force, as melodrama, as orientalism, as decadence, as mysticism, at moments as nihilism, and they remain noisy with uneasiness and terror. Each reader must decide for himself when they speak meaningfully or when they offer nothing but the absurd echoes of the void.

Hemingway said that when you spoke about an emotion, you lost it forever. Isak Dinesen, less of a pessimist, said something similar when she wrote that all sorrows can be borne if they are put into a story or if a story is told about them. Civilized man has generally encouraged the release of catharsis. Hemingway, however suggests the ambivalence of the modern writer who is shaken by a coldness out there in a world which no longer believes, where ghosts neither settle under beds nor upon altars. More than any other twentieth-century writer, James allows his characters to maintain the active internal experience which is their peculiar birthright, and he does so by allowing them the integrity of their silences.

Silence in Henry James may not be the elusive figure in the carpet, but it spreads itself out behind the weave of surface decoration, behind gilt and ormolu, behind repartee and plain talk. In his fiction the retreat from the word, from more obvious phenomena, and from modalities of explicit action, provides a sustained code for forces which constantly inspire and threaten the imaginative characters who make their way through a supersophisticated modern world.

2 The Prelude to Silence: Roderick Hudson and The American

"Rome is an evil word in my mother's vocabulary, to be said in a whisper, as you'd say 'damnation.' "

Roderick Hudson

The road from New England to Rome has held terrors for sons of the Puritans, for in the center of an alien Christendom threads of spirituality and gold hopelessly intertwine. Cardinals might face a miraculously rich *baldacchino* and sit upon splendid thrones as they beatify an Iberian mystic who taught that the path to God was the negative way, where everything is cut away—splendor, power, affection, hope, and love itself. The irony that all roads lead to Rome, even the *via negativa* of John of the Cross, might have puzzled those people in Henry James who were notoriously from Woollett, Northampton, and Boston. To them Roman Catholicism and its capital cities could represent the overwrought and the overextended, and in *The Ambassadors*, at least for Strether's friend, the fearsome—"the Catholic Church, the enemy, the monster of bulging eyes and far-reaching quivering, groping tentacles—was exactly society, exactly the multiplication of shibboleths, exactly the discrimination of types and tones, exactly, in short, Europe."[1] Rome supplied such images of redundant excess for these people, and it provides the extreme metaphor of attractive positivism in *Roderick Hudson*. Surely there can be few silences inside the basilica of Saint Peter, where even at moments of attenuated holiness, the condition would seem a riot of spirituality.

The difficulty of extracting the soul of art or religion from the gilt is both the artist's and the believer's task, and in Rome it seems an easy thing to worship false gods. Roderick Hudson fails to value the

New England understatement which he leaves behind. He believes that he moves toward artistic growth as he heads for the plenitude that is Rome, and yet he ends artistically vacant. The more his life informs with phenomena, the more devitalized the young artist becomes, until finally, at the pinnacle of activity in the great city, he asks his friend: "Did you ever hear of inspiration? Mine is dead." And he claims that Rowland, who took him to Rome, killed it.[2] His position reverses that of Milly Theale in *The Wings of the Dove*; in Venice, a city which suggests an entirely different metaphor, she withdraws from life, goes completely quiet, retreats to the chamber of her *palazzo* and faces the wall. But she experiences the vibrant "adventure of not stirring."[3] Roderick Hudson begins as the most energetic and voluble Jamesian hero, but he ends chillingly lifeless.

Perhaps neither very complex nor very engaging, *Roderick Hudson* establishes structural relationships which recur, with increasing sophistication, throughout the later novels. Two antipodal female characters, one as reticent as Mary Garland, the other as vibrant a polyglot as Christina Light, set up the dialectic as they fight for the fairish, goodish, youngish man torn between the spirit and the flesh. Upon an equally materialistic field Fleda Vetch battles the monumentality of Mona Brigstock and loses, but Milly Theale and finally Maggie Verver claim victories over essentially positivistic rivals.

In *Roderick Hudson* the focuses of Mary Garland and Northampton may muster insufficient force against their attractive foils, but James intended such force. In his New York Edition "Preface" he writes of Northampton:

> Pathetic, as we say, on the other hand, no doubt, to reperusal, the manner in which the evocation, so far as attempted, of the small New England town of my first two chapters, fails of intensity—if intensity, in such a connection, had been indeed to be looked for. *Could* I verily, by the terms of my little plan, have "gone in" for it at the best, and even though one of those terms was the projection, for my fable, at the outset, of some more or less vivid antithesis to a state of civilization providing for "art."[4]

And of Mary Garland he writes:

The difficulty had been from the first that I required my antithesis to Christina Light, one of the main terms of the subject. One is ridden by the law that antithesis, to be efficient, shall be both direct and complete. Directness seemed to fail unless Mary should be, so to speak, "plain," Christina being essentially so "coloured"; and completeness seemed to fail unless she too should have her potency.[5]

Although Mary Garland would go with Everyman to the grave, she remains too undefined. The potency of the plain woman will emerge only in the late novels, when to some extent James abandons the visual metaphor and begins expression with the more ambiguously reflective modalities of the unspoken.

More artistic inspiration comes from Northampton than from Rome. Whenever described, the sleepy New England town is presented in terms of absences, in terms of what it denies rather than what it provides the imagination. On the first page the narrator reports that Rowland Mallett's cousin's "misfortunes were three in number: first, she had lost her husband; second, she had lost her money (or the greater part of it); and third, she lived at Northampton, Massachusetts" (pp. 1–2). And when Gloriani marvels at the young figure "Thirst," he says:

> "Was this done in America?" he asked.
> "In a square white wooden house in Northampton, Massachusetts," Roderick answered.
> "Dear old white wooden houses!" said Miss Blanchard.
> "If you could do as well as this there," said Singleton, blushing and smiling, "one might say that really you had only to lose by coming to Rome." [pp. 109–10]

Despite his blushes, Singleton is right. Roderick Hudson's artistic sensibility deadens as it moves from a world of spare phenomena, with neither models nor apparent inspiration. In Northampton he brims with a "boyish garrulity" which he soon loses in Europe. When searching for Hudson at the end, Rowland "challenged the stupid silence to tell him something about his friend. Some of those places had evidently not been open in months. The silence everywhere was horrible; it seemed to be a conscious symbol of calamity" (p. 477).

In his "Preface" James writes that the novelist, as "to due density in his material [would] have found little enough in Northampton, Mass., to tackle."[6] But if the New England town might mean "intense" absences, the polarity of the Italian capital would offer nothing less than plenitude. When Mary Garland confronts Mallett with her distrust of European excess, she asks him, "Is *this* what you call life? . . . Saint Peter's—all this splendor, all Rome—pictures, ruins, statues, beggars, monks" (p. 305). He promises that she will see "an immense number of beautiful things," but she apprehensively replies that hers has been the "duty of sitting in the white-washed meetinghouse" (p. 307).

When Hudson first settles in Rome he prefers a quiet spot and retreats to the Villa Ludovisi, "where the colossal mask of the famous Juno looks out with blank eyes from that dusky corner" (p. 77). Here he begins his statue of Adam, under the influence of this vaguely defined, blank-eyed deity—the generative "veiled face of his Muse which [the artist] is condemned forever and all anxiously to study," in the words of the "Preface." When, however, Christina Light enters the scene, only for a moment, and drifts past the artist, the veil is lifted. Roderick sketches a picture which "represented the Juno as to the position of the head, the brow, the broad fillet across the hair but the eyes, the mouth, the physiognomy were a vivid portrait of the young girl with the poodle" (p. 89). Christina Light fills in the blank spaces of artistic inspiration, draws the artist closer to the world, and the decline begins. She provides recorded phenomena where before there had been anxious absence, and critics have called her a muse,[7] as they have termed Rome inspirational. But what the lovely woman gives with one hand, she takes away with the other. Roderick Hudson takes as consort too fleshly a muse. The first figure he produces, the Hellenistic Δίψα or "Thirst," clearly an apprentice piece, holds great promise. Done "without models or resources," it turns out "remarkable," "exquisitely rendered." It represents a drinking youth, "Hylas or Narcissus, Paris or Endymion" (pp. 16–18), all young men who, like Hudson, met their particular destructions because they loved too physical beauty.

Hudson goes to Rome, where at first he retreats from the city and takes to his studio, "a huge, empty room with a vaulted ceiling" (p. 90). There he works the finest figure of his career, his "Adam." The life-sized statue "partook, really, of the miraculous," and it was said "he never surpassed it afterward" (p. 95). But as Hudson stays on in Rome, he moves out of the vaulted chamber and grows attached to the physical splendor of the city, of its celebrities, and of Christina Light, who seems to be its genius. The "Eve," his next work, was finished in one month, and "the feat was extraordinary, as well as the statue" (p. 96). The "feat" of the speed gets more attention than the work itself, which is noted as if in afterthought. Nonetheless, done in a bare studio after only a momentary glimpse of Christina Light, the work maintains a visionary aspect.

> Roderick lost his temper, time and time again, with his models, who offered but a gross, degenerate image of his splendid ideal; but his ideal, as he assured Rowland, became gradually such a fixed, vivid presence, that he had only to shut his eyes to behold a creature far more to his purpose than the poor girl who stood posturing at forty sous an hour. [p. 96]

Until this point, the center of artistic energy remains unseen, distinctly apart from worldly phenomena, the inspiration of the blank-eyed Juno in the removed garden.

Hudson finds himself increasingly reduced by Rome and he becomes a worshiper of incarnate beauty. His methods begin to change. He forms a head of Christina Light meticulously and adoringly, "reproducing line for line and curve for curve" (p. 169). He derives no inspiration from the unseen and he becomes an elegant copyist. Miss Light herself suggests that he place her statue under a painting by Sassoferrato, a minor Renaissance artist of whom it has been said that "his free copies after Raphael, Titian, Perugino and other masters are occasionally of great merit; being far superior to his original works."[8] James himself had earlier spoken of Sassoferrato—"The artist has nothing to offer but 'finish', but he offers this in elegant profusion."[9] The statue is different in kind from the Adam.

> The bust was in fact a very happy performance, and Roderick had risen to the level of his subject. It was thoroughly a portrait, and not a vague fantasy executed on a graceful theme, as the busts of pretty woman, in modern sculpture, are apt to be. The resemblance was deep and vivid; there was extreme fidelity of detail. [p. 165]

The "Adam," done during the first days in Rome, "partook of the miraculous"; here the depiction of ideal physical beauty is called "a very happy performance." At this point Hudson claims he will next make a "Christ"—but he never will. Then Christina enters, and Miss Blanchard, uneasy spokesman of white-walled New England, tells him, "you ought to make a Judas" (p. 106). Christina Light eventually understands that she means betrayal to the artist. Finally she cries that she represents the world, the "Splendid, beautiful, powerful, interesting world. . . . I am corrupt, corruptible, corruption!" (pp. 370–71). After his first encounter with her, something seemingly divine made something surely fleshly, Hudson first falters and then falls. Only a few pages after his inspiration by Miss Light's beauty, he himself cries, "I have stuck a shallow! I have been sailing bravely but . . . Nothing comes; all of a sudden I hate things" (pp. 114–15).

The execution of Hudson's final figure forcefully demonstrates his decline. He produces a bust of his mother, "a charming piece of quaintness: a little demure, thin-lipped old lady, with her head on one side, and the prettiest wrinkles in the world" (p. 330). Before falling in love with Christina Light, Hudson spoke of grand abstractions—"They shall be divine forms. They shall be Beauty; they shall be Wisdom; they shall be Power; they shall be Genius; they shall be Daring. That's all the Greek divinities were" (p. 108). But the energy runs off. He follows the biological lines of the goddess of physical beauty and then he works to reproduce the wrinkles of "a sort of fairy godmother" (p. 330). Viewers—Mallett among them—cluck happily over this final work, but the description given of it is so faintly positive that it seems to devastate.

> In the bust of Mrs. Hudson there was something almost touching. . . . The poor lady's small, timorous face had certainly no great character, but Roderick had produced its sweetness, its mildness, its minuteness, its maternal passion, with the most unerring art. It was perfectly unflattered, and yet admirably tender; it was the poetry of fidelity. [p. 330]

Such comes of fidelity to the world of Christina Light: the timorous, the sweet, the minute and mild, the worn and somewhat dessicated, the almost touching—but none of the visionary force which excited the artist in Northampton. Three years before publishing *Roderick Hudson* Henry James wrote a review article on the recent Metropolitan Museum acquisitions. The description of "Mrs. Hudson" seems to echo his disparagement of some of the pieces he saw in New York.

We doubt that the mouth and chin of small local authority were ever more inexorably fixed in their pursey identity than these comfortable attributes of this most respectable Dutchman. It seems almost hyperbolical to talk of Van der Helst as an *artist*; genuine painter as he was, his process is not so much the common, leisurely, critical return upon reality and truth as a bonded and indissoluble union with it.[10]

Union with Christina Light may be only incidentally sexual; it is a more basic sensual world—even when expressed by the mildness of his own recorded mother—to which Hudson unites himself. In the heart of the world's classical capital, Hudson shifts from Hellenism and idealism to a cautious, sentimental, second-rank Dutch realism. He regresses back home, back north, back all the way to mother. He ends engaged in experience, but with no creative chasm—Singleton refers to "his beautiful completeness. 'Complete,' that's what he is" (p. 172)—initiated and then experienced in the fulness of what he thought would make him a great artist. The nuances and the "faintest hints of life" of "The Art of Fiction" are swept away to make place for the extraordinary full table that Christina Light and Rome both offer.

Roderick Hudson ends with Mary Garland as the center of attention. Rowland waits on her and says, to close, "I assure you I am most patient," but she remains an unconvincing heroine. In the "Preface" James regrets that "the spell of attraction" of "Mary Garland doesn't indubitably convince us."[11] This quiet Mary, from a place called West Nazareth, shifts in the background, ready to enliven the creative imagination, but she remains too far in the background. She will be reworked again and again until the essentially plain woman attains surpassing power. In her and in *Roderick Hudson* as a whole are seeds of antipositivism that will relate to a major theme—that the surest way to meet life may be to withdraw from a life that, however attractive, is too rich, too full, and consequently the path to emptiness.

An immense distance separates the Italian capital from the French. Rome's vehemently masculine worldliness—expressed by its pagan heritage, heroic scale, and muscular Michelangelesque sensuality, has little to do with the misty atmosphere of the city sliced by a dreamlike river. *Roderick Hudson's* immaturity regarded aesthetic materialism as the greatest value of Europe. Yet only in his most callow days in the Louvre does Christopher Newman read the physical embarrassment of riches as the essence of Paris, and in time Notre Dame casts a shadow entirely different from that before Saint Peter's. Ultimately the dim gothic cathedral and not the palatial museum best provides the atmosphere for an awakening consciousness. In Paris another American faces the silent and essentially uncolored, and he recognizes unmistakable potency.

In 1904 *The Golden Bowl* would present a quiet heroine who renounces nothing. She does not, like other of James's heroines, enter a convent, return to the frigidity of a dilettante husband, sit in a dim parlor with needle and a morsel of fancywork, die of a nameless disease, or even return to America. She regains her husband and embraces him in love and terror at the end. *The American* develops some patterns and concerns of the far more complex later novels—particularly the linking of silence with spirituality and aspects of religion. But although later novels develop silence as complex force, in *The American* it provides little more than stylish denouement, a graceful renunciation which eases and perhaps encourages the withdrawal from life.

Although *The American* closes with impressive silences—Valentin's, Claire's, the Bellegardes', and Newman's, the book begins with talk. Christopher Newman meets a not quite respectable young copyist in the Louvre, and the young woman and her father offer to teach him French conversation.

> "I can't fancy myself chattering French!" said Newman with a laugh. "And yet, I suppose that the more a man knows the better."
> "Monsieur expresses that very happily. *Hélas, oui!*"
> "I suppose it would help me a great deal, knocking about Paris, to know the language."[12]

This questionable father and daughter tell the American that success and the conversation of the "best society" are closely linked, and they promise that Newman will "speak like an angel." Yet the preposterous scientificity of the passage near the end of the first chapter hints at the irony.

> Newman had never reflected upon philological processes. His chief impression with regard to ascertaining those mysterious correlatives of his familiar English vocables which were current in this extraordinary city of Paris was that it was simply a

matter of a good deal of unwonted and rather ridiculous muscular effort on his part. [p. 17]

Christopher Newman holds the views of a materialist whose money
sits comfortably in the background. He enters the salons of Paris—
enters the world—and goes off in search of the right language, the
athletic talk and clever words which will allow him to get what he
wants. Talk, however, does not carry him far. The Bellegardes present
an impeccable aristocratic reserve and Christopher Newman is no match
for them, however emphatically the Nioches might promise the contrary. Power and some purity inform the silences in this early novel,
but speech comes from a corrupt tongue. The tutelage offered to the
American would seem the wrong kind of instruction.

> The language spoken by M. Nioche was a singular com-
> pound, which I shrink from the attempt to reproduce in its
> integrity. He had apparently once possessed a certain knowl-
> edge of English, and his accent was oddly tinged with the
> cockneyism of the British metropolis. But his learning had
> grown rusty with disuse, and his vocabulary was defective and
> capricious. He had repaired it with large patches of French,
> with words anglicized by a process of his own, and with native
> idioms literally translated. The result, in the form which he
> in all humility presented it, would scarcely be comprehensible
> to the reader. [p. 60]

The silences in *The American* come late, the first at the end of the
nineteenth chapter of this twenty-six-chapter book. Valentin de Bellegarde, the friend to Christopher Newman, is dying of a bullet wound
received in a duel over the somewhat less than honorable Mademoiselle
Noémie. He tells Newman to discover the secret of the house of
Bellegarde.

> The words died away in a long, soft groan. Newman stood up,
> deeply impressed, not knowing what to say; his heart beating
> violently. "Thank you," he said at last. "I am much obliged."
> But Valentin seemed not to hear him; he remained silent, and
> his silence continued. [pp. 350–51]

Soon Claire de Cintré departs for the convent at Fleurieres, as a religious of the Carmelite order. She withdraws from the world and takes a vow of silence. Newman later hears the impressive chant of the nuns in their procession—"It began softly, but it presently grew louder, and as it increased it became more of a wail and a dirge. It was the chant of the Carmelite nuns, their only human utterance" (p. 421).

Then Newman stops the Bellegardes as they walk and he presents Madame de Bellegarde and her son with a copy of a note that proves their complicity in Monsieur de Bellegarde's murder. The report of the note might destroy the whole family; Newman watches the old woman.

> The expression of her face was such that he fancied at first that she was smiling; but he went and stood in front of her, and saw that her elegant features were distorted by agitation. He saw, however, equally, that she was resisting her agitation with all the rigor of her inflexible will, and there was nothing like either fear or submission in her stony stare. [pp. 430–31]

The son turns to the mother and pleads, "What shall I say?" "There is only one thing to say," said the marquise. "That it was really not worth while to have interrupted our walk" (pp. 433–34). They withdraw from Paris, take retreat in the country, and leave the final silence to Newman. In his hand he holds evidence which might win revenge and then he tosses it into the fire.

> "It is most provoking," said Mrs. Tristram, "to hear you talk of the 'charge' when the charge is burnt up. It is quite consumed?" she asked, glancing at the fire.
>
> Newman assured her that there was nothing left of it.
>
> "Well then," she said, "I suppose there is no harm in saying that you probably did not make them so very uncomfortable. My impression would be that since, as you say, they defied you, it was because they believed that, after all, you would never really come to the point. Their confidence, after counsel taken of each other, was not in their innocence, nor in their talent for bluffing things off; it was in your remarkable good nature! You see they were right."
>
> Newman instinctively turned to see if the little paper was in fact consumed; but there was nothing left of it. [pp. 472–73]

It is the biggest fire in Henry James, except perhaps for the one that burns Poynton to the ground.

Silence claims all the figures in the novel—Valentin, Claire, Madame de Bellegarde and her son, and then Newman himself, providing each a dignified exit; yet inevitably an element of grimness may displease the reader who sees the life that might have been lived, all lost. The stylish quiet is a dusty affair here. Nonetheless, silence in *The American* gains resonance by being merged with aristocracy and European Catholicism, both founded upon inexorable rule.

The housekeeper, Mrs. Bread, refers to the Carmelites and speaks of "the rule of the house" and says "there is no rule so strict" (p. 412). She could be referring to the house of Bellegarde, with its precept that will not allow Madame de Cintré to reveal why she cannot marry the American. The old marquise ranges about like the mother superior of an order, and Claire speaks, in religious terms, of duty to family— "What had she meant by her feeling being a kind of religion? It was the religion simply of the family laws, the religion of which her implacable little mother was the high priestess" (p. 370). High priestess or mother superior, the Marquise de Bellegarde stands out of the world, and her house, when Newman first sees it, "was all in shade; it answered to Newman's conception of a convent" (p. 57). She begins at the beginning only a little less cloistered than her daughter at the end. When Newman first questions the marquise about Paris, she responds, "I can't say I know it. I know my house—I know my friends—I don't know Paris" (p. 171). Christopher Newman does not appreciate that the distance from the aristocratic convent to the religious one is not great. Silence and withdrawal are essential to a European tradition which he just barely suspects, that of a great world removed from worldliness. At the end Claire says she is going "Where I shall give no more pain and suspect no more evil. I am going out of the world." "Out of the world?" questions Newman. "Out of the world," she repeats (p. 365).

These same words describe Christopher Newman at a crucial moment. When, after traveling for months around Europe, dipping into London society and continental pleasures, he learns from Mrs. Tristram that Claire de Cintré has taken the veil, the convent's stillness strikes him as hideous. He believes what Mrs. Bread tells him—"They tell me it's the most dreadful, sir; of all the nuns in Christendom the Carmelites are the worst. You may say they are not human, sir; they make you give up everything—forever" (p. 374). Then Newman meets his quiet epiphanies, first outside the convent and then in the great cathedral.

At the intersection of two of these streets stood the house of the Carmelites—a dull, plain edifice, with a high-shouldered blank wall all around it. . . . The place looked dumb, deaf, inanimate. The pale, dead, discolored wall stretched beneath it, far down the empty side street—a vista without human figure. Newman stood there a long time; there were no passers; he was free to gaze his fill. This seemed the goal of his journey; it was what he had come for. It was a strange satisfaction, and yet it was a satisfaction; the barren stillness of the place seemed to be his own release from ineffectual longing. [pp. 467–68]

He wanders from the convent and finds himself at Notre Dame.

He crossed one of the bridges and stood a moment in the empty place before the great cathedral; then he went in beneath the grossly-imaged portals. He wandered some distance up the nave and sat down in the splendid dimness. He sat a long time; he heard far-away bells chiming off, at long intervals, to the rest of the world. He was very tired; this was the best place he could be in. He said no prayers; he had no prayers to say. He had nothing to be thankful for, and he had nothing to ask; nothing to ask, because now he must take care of himself. But a cathedral offers a very various hospitality, and Newman sat in his place, because while he was there he was out of the world. [p. 468]

The impulse at the end is similar to that of the shadowy, mysterious chambers of many symbolist paintings. Christopher Newman ends, like the marquise and her daughter, out of the world, in a quiet place, with no words. The moment brings him to reluctant grace, his education in Europe nears completion, and the bottom drops out of his revenge.

Those who insist that Christopher Newman renounces all that is essential to Europe ignore the close pattern that exists between his actions and Madame de Cintré's final religious retreat. Newman finally does not reject Europe; he begins to be assimilated by it and by the silences of its two greatest institutions. After he makes the realization, Europe serves no longer as a simply odd expression of America to him. He at first thought that the important difference was obvious phenomena and talk, but the difference evolves as a complex silence and an awareness of almost unrecognizable and certainly unnameable impulses.

This brash young man begins to perceive the "interior spectacle" of which some of the symbolists spoke. He traveled around Europe and checked off 470 churches in his Baedeker, but at the end he finds Europe in one quiet pew.

Christopher Newman went on the Grand Tour to learn what Europe was about, to gain a speech that spoke best, forcefully to exercise freedom. To him Europe meant plenitudes—the most enriched society, the most expressive languages, the most ornate religion. The power of Europe, however, evolves as the antithesis of the exteriority he sought. At first the Faubourg St. Germain baffled him as a quarter "whose houses present to the outer world a face as impassive and as suggestive of the concentration of privacy within as the blank walls of Eastern seraglios. Newman thought it a queer way for rich people to live; his idea of grandeur was a splendid facade, diffusing its brillancy outward too" (p. 56). He comes to feel the antithetical grandeur of the retreated and the bare—an energy which exists out of the world, alien to the experience of a muscular American materialist. Christopher Newman takes a brief novitiate in Paris, among the Bellegardes and in Notre Dame, and he leaves changed—"At last he got up and came out of the darkening church; not with the elastic step of a man who had won a victory or taken a resolve, but strolling soberly, like a good-natured man who is still a little ashamed" (p. 469).

The quieting of Europe is a delicate matter. The near-pagan contradictions of institutional Roman Catholicism lose their intensity as spirituality approaches monastic rule and, in later fiction, mystic sensibility; from the first a subtle oriental fragrance seems to linger. Rome's baroque redundancy slowly transforms into the blank walls of Eastern palaces as an alien wordless life counters Western positivism. In James's last completed novel, The Golden Bowl, the metaphorical focus of Maggie Verver's consciousness becomes at one moment "some strange tall tower of ivory, or perhaps some wonderful, beautiful, but outlandish pagoda,"[13] and such associations begin to move beyond symbolist concerns. Havelock Ellis, in his 1931 Introduction to À Rebours, speaks of Huysmans as "at once the ultramodern child of a refined civilization and the victim of nostalgia for ascetic mediaevalism"[14] and adds a note about a persistent attraction to the East, as if to "the cat, whose outward repose of Buddhistic contemplation envelops a highly-strung nervous system, while its capacity to enjoy the refinements of human civilization comports a large measure of spiritual freedom and ferocity."[15]

James shared the symbolist's distrust of materialism and of positivism, but he would never belong to their café movement. Although, finally, *The American* suggests the movement's fertile silences and subtle orientalism, much of his subsequent work remains apart from the universality of their mainstream. His more indoor sensibility never shared their belief in ready truth, accessible "through the poet's soul as through nature in her various forms—landscape, water, soul, and perfume."[16] The mysterious truth he pursued had little to do with the generality of nature, of collective unconscious, or of myth. Consequently, James's position belongs, for a time, between that of the gregarious anti-positivists and that of those more alienated figures whose more evanescent awareness drew them to isolation and nihilism. The monastic murmurs of early Henry James begin to move *à rebours*, against the grain, as they betray an increasingly esoteric fascination with the remotest pulses of life. A wordless universe begins to unfold behind closed doors, and at times it almost completely abandons the potential refreshment which symbolists read into symbiosis with nature. It is as a near-decadent that James was to write some of his most powerful tales, where silent voices speak with the persistent accent of perversity.

3 The Scent of Decadence: The Ghostly Tales

Perhaps the notoriously dignified presence of Henry James has discouraged his association with the extremes of pampered delicacy in the aesthetic eighties. G. L. Van Roosbroeck evokes the stereotype as well as anyone when he describes the decadent making his way down the boulevard.

> . . . fatally pale, disquietingly pale. His lips were too red, his wandering eyes circled with kohl. . . . His hair, vaguely curly, was cut like that of the angels on a Botticelli painting; his white hands were covered with rings, on which sparkled the fire of magic stones, of onyx, of topaz and rubies. His soft, silken necktie—delicate lilac and silver—was knotted with consummate taste, low and loose around a bare throat, à la Byron.[1]

The Master seated marmoreally in the Sussex study seems to have had little to do with things Byronic or with the satanically seraphic concerns of those who made their way along the Left Bank at midnight. When, however, The Yellow Book appeared in 1894, with drawings by Beardsley and with poems by questionable poets, Henry James's work was prominently among them. James's "The Death of a Lion" headed up the inaugural issue and his "The Coxon Fund" closed the second issue.[2] The publication was called the folio of "aesthetic depravity, of the veil trembling on the brink of revelation, of superfine consciousness active before impression."[3] And the cry went out that James had "been in bad company" and had "become one of the Yellow Book Clique." James himself wrote to the editor that "I hate too much the horrid aspect and company of the whole publication."[4] He had in fact hated the aspect for almost a decade, at least as far back as when he uneasily entertained Count Robert de Montesquiou, the "Prince of Decadence," who, four years later, was to supply a model for Huysmans's Des Esseintes in À Rebours.[5] Nonetheless, he kept up his association and admitted that he was "to be intimately, conspicuously associated with the 2nd number"—and with two more numbers after that.

When Oscar Wilde was arrested in 1895, the newspaper headlines announced "YELLOW BOOK UNDER HIS ARM." H. Montgomery Hyde reports that the yellow-covered volume was Pierre Louÿs's Aphrodite; nonetheless, the mix-up killed The Yellow Book, as it almost killed its publisher, John Lane.[6] The scandal ended James's association with the decadents, but he had rubbed shoulders with them for some years, and much that he wrote accommodated itself to the adventure of their fin-de-siècle refinement.

The sensational stereotype of the decadent is misleading. Addressing the attacks on the first Yellow Book, Max Beerbohm, in the second number, followed James's story with a letter which defined decadence as characterized by "paradox and marivaudage, lassitude, a love of horror and all unusual things, a love of argot, and archaism and the mysteries of style."[7] Beerbohm's satire in part derives from the paradox, argot ("marivaudage") and the stylistic mysteries of his own work, but his definition of decadence is serious, and it comes close to the expression of James's tales. Indeed, much of the later fiction might be seen as aligning itself with Arthur Symons's more complex definition in his groundbreaking 1893 "The Decadent Movement in Literature":

> . . . it is no doubt decadence; it has all the qualities that mark the end of great periods, the qualities that we find in the Greek, the Latin, decadence: an intense self-consciousness, a restless curiosity in research, an oversubtilizing refinement upon refinement, a spiritual and moral perversity. If what we call the classic is indeed the supreme art—those qualities of perfect simplicity, perfect sanity, perfect proportion, the supreme qualities—then this representative literature of today, interesting, beautiful, novel as it is, is really a new and beautiful and interesting disease.[8]

Although far from Des Esseintes's overpowering display of racial
exhaustion, later Jamesian men share that decadent's awareness of "certain
whisperings of thought so soft and low, certain avowals so gently
murmured, so brokenly expressed, that the ear catching them was left
hesitating, passing on to the mind langours stirred by the mystery of
sound divined rather than heard."[9] Even the relatively robust Lambert
Strether in *The Ambassadors* has such moments, and when he finally
awakens to the truth, he awakens completely and seems able to read
the pulses in the air. When he pays a visit to Maria Gostrey's apartment,
he stands there for a moment, quiet, still, taking in the room. Gostrey
breaks out with "Yes, she has been here." Not only does the gentleman
have the ability to divine truth from airborne whispers, but the lady
can tell what he so quietly senses. Common scenes in Henry James,
they invite parody and they get parody. As early as 1904 Frank Moore
Colby was to offer a characteristic dialogue of two preternaturally acute
young Jamesians.

> "If—" she sparkled.
> "If!" he asked. He had lurched from the meaning for a
> moment.
> "I might"—she replied abundantly.
> His eye had eaten the meaning—"Me!" he gloriously burst.
> "Precisely," she thrilled. "How splendidly you *do*
> understand."[10]

Verlaine's lines, "Car nous voulons la nuance encore/ Pas la couleur,
rien que la nuance" ["Never the Color, always the Shade,/ always the
nuance is supreme"], which both Huysmans and Symons discuss,[11] get
near the heart of the decadent sensibility. Neither so frail nor so shut-
tered as the caped poseurs, James shared their revolt against positivity
and, in a somewhat subdued manner, many of their darker mannerisms.

In 1868 Théophile Gautier spoke about Baudelaire's "style of decadence"; the words might apply to the late Henry James. Gautier said
that Baudelaire's

> . . . art arrived at the point of extreme maturity yielded by
> the slanting suns of aged civilizations: an ingenious compli-
> cated style, full of shades and of research, constantly pushing
> back the boundaries of speech, borrowing from all the tech-
> nical vocabularies, taking colour from all palettes and notes

from all keyboards, struggling to render what is the most inexpressible in thought, what is vague and most elusive in outlines
of form, listening to translate the subtle confidences of neu-
rosis, the dying confessions of passion grown depraved, and
the strange hallucinations of the obsession which is turning
to madness. The style of decadence is the ultimate utterance
of the Word, summoned to final expression and driven to its
last hiding-place.[12]

Although James never was enamored, like Baudelaire, of the phos-
phorescence of putrescence, there are moments, particularly in the later
tales—in "The Altar of the Dead," "Maud-Evelyn," "The Beast in the
Jungle," and "The Jolly Corner" most notably—where strange "hallucinations of the obsession" and near-madness grow out of morbidly
developed anti-positivism. The sickly and the ghostly, the dying and
the dead carry the fiction to the fringes of life, while attention to
nuance, to whispers, to argot, to intense curiosity, to aggravated self-
consciousness, to over-subtilization, refinement, and complexity all
liken James's style to that of the decadents. Ultimately, a persistent
odor of decay brings him close to their uneasy themes, and although
the tales may not provide the breviary of decadence which Huysmans's
work did, certain heroes remove themselves from life as far as did Des
Esseintes. They find pleasure engaging themselves, literally or figura-
tively, to ghastly creatures who haunt—even when transformed into
dove-like shadows—throughout the fiction.

A writer can attempt things in tales that would fail miserably in
extended works. Tzvetan Todorov writes, "the public prefers novels to
tales, long books to short texts, not because length is taken as criterion
of value, but because there is not time, in reading a short work, to
forget it is only 'literature' and not 'life.' "[13] The "limitation" Todorov
discusses provides the story-writer with a luxury: the reader, for ten or
twenty pages, may accept extreme strokes requiring a Coleridgean "sus-
pension of disbelief for the moment which constitutes the poetic faith."[14]
in part because the reader hardly ever forgets the "literate" other-than-
life quality of the short tale. Were ghosts to roam the halls for 400
pages, the poetic faith might snap long before the narration got to its
end. The short tale allowed James to experiment with intensified concerns which would inform the greater part of his work in the novel,
but which would demand more muted, more "realistic" treatment in
the lengthy genre.

In the view of Todorov, James's ghosts represent "the essence [that] is never present except as a ghost, that is, absence par excellence."[15] The ghosts emerge as palpable nuances and demonstrate that hyper-attenuated obsessions can allure, corrupt, madden, and kill. They ambiguously present symbolist concerns, most present perhaps as "literature," or as symbol, rather than as "life," to extend Todorov's distinction, and they brighten as the tales move toward the late period, as the silences gain potency, and as the vacancies become more focused centers. Although few ghosts people the novels, in *The Portrait of a Lady* an important one appears which not all readers take seriously. When Isabel Archer arrives at Gardencourt, she asks that her cousin show her the ghost of the house. Ralph, smiling but as narrow-shouldered, weary, and manipulative as any decadent, responds sadly enough.

> "It has never been seen by a young, happy, innocent person like you. You must have suffered first, have suffered greatly, have gained some miserable knowledge. In that way your eyes are opened to it. I saw it long ago."[16]

At the moment of her cousin's death, the ghost appears to Isabel, or so it seems.

> It seemed to her for an instant that he was standing there—a dim, hovering figure in the dimness of the room. She stared a moment; she saw his white face—his kind eyes; then she saw there was nothing. She was not afraid; she was only sure. She went out of her room, and in her certainty passed through dark corridors and down a flight of oaken steps that shone in vague light of a hall-window. Outside Ralph's door she stopped a moment, listening; but she seemed to hear only the hush that filled it.[17]

As Martha Banta writes, "The veridical hallucination that comes to Isabel at the moment of Ralph Touchett's death need not be read as an actual ghost appearance; it can remain a finely handled poetic truth that measures Isabel's deepest point of awareness."[18] Surely Isabel's almost Baudelairean hallucination is complex. An examination of the growing metaphor of ghostly forces in the tales may help demonstrate that hushes fulfill and ghosts appear when imaginative people make discoveries about unsuspected, unspeaking potencies.

"The Madonna of the Future" (1879), although not a literal ghost tale, strongly demonstrates preoccupation with Todorov's "absence par excellence." For twenty years the painter Theobald holds the image of a perfect madonna in his teeming brain, but, as is finally discovered, for that entire period his canvas has remained absolutely untouched— "a canvas that was a mere dead blank, cracked and discolored by time."[19] Nonetheless, that blank canvas serves as the center of Theobald's life. Although he fails, Theobald displays more passion than the lot of pitying onlookers, than the sympathetic narrator pausing on the Grand Tour, than the aging and sometimes lovely Serafina, than Serafina's crass artisan lover. Despite the uneasy vacancy at the heart of his story, Theobald seem vital and the others do not. His first words speak vigorously of the absent energy which he alone discerns.

> "I've known Florence long, sir, but I've never known her so lovely as to-night. It's as if the ghosts of her past were abroad in the empty streets. The present is sleeping; the past hovers about us like a dream made visible." ["Madonna," III, 13]

Critics may condemn Theobald and deride the sensibility which prefers exquisite contemplation of a blank canvas to an affair with the woman considered the most beautiful in Italy,[20] and perhaps they are right. Yet in 1875 James had written of talent and practice united and wedded to another incarnate expression of beauty. Roderick Hudson accepted the actuality that Christina Light offered him and ended up vacant. Hudson may represent the artist who does; Theobald, he who does not—the persistent monastic spirit who chooses the madonna over the Venus. With a dramatic leap or fall from a cliff, Hudson dies in a bleak setting; Theobald, after learning that his ideal beauty has coarsened into an aging peasant woman, dies, with a sigh merging into silence.

> The eyes and lips of the great portraits seemed to smile in ineffable scorn of the dejected pretender who had dreamed of competing with their triumphant authors; the celestial candor, even, of the Madonna in the Chair, as we paused in perfect silence before her, was tinged with the sinister irony of the woman of Leonardo. Perfect silence indeed marked our whole

progress—the silence of a deep farewell. ["Madonna," III, 48–49]

Yet James does not sharply condemn Theobald, in spite of the artist's adolescent maturity. Theobald dies after knowing something of life—its passion, pity, and potential for love. He lives sufficiently, after having read symbolist pulses in the air, and after having spoken of them.

James will tell Theobald's story repeatedly, and it will evolve. Structural repetition of the blank canvas will stir more aggressive ghosts, and even such a late tale as "The Beast in the Jungle" has something in common with "The Madonna of the Future." Two men dream of an ultimate experience; both wait a lifetime in some sort of lovely hiatus. Women appear and offer themselves, first as lovers and then as quiet handmaidens who attend upon the waiting, for the muse to descend or for the beast to leap. With "The Beast in the Jungle," however, the energy of blankness stirs powerful loins and materializes aggressively as a quasi-occult presence which throws John Marcher down onto a tomb. In 1879 Theobald still demonstrates more or less healthy vigor, although his descendants will make less and less claim to his Mediterranean vitality. Theobald is distinguished as an early hero who engages himself not to the essence of Christina Light or American materialism, but to a symbolist ideal—here confused with a physical woman, but less confused in later tales. "The Beast in the Jungle" seems far less tolerant of the life manqué. In "The Madonna of the Future" the hero dies, but not before being cast into a relatively positive light; the tale closes with the refrain of Seraphina's lover, the man who compromised his art, created, made love, succeeded. The narrator hears his blaring call as he sells animal sculptures in the streets—"Cats and monkeys, monkeys and cats; all human life is there" ("Madonna," III, 52). By 1903, however, a reversal has occurred and the tiger of the void, not the street-vendor's plaster cat, represents the most vicious negativism.

"The Real Thing" (1883) presents, more classically than any other tale, James's distrust of the apparent positivism which Christina Light represents. Here an artist needs models for his work. The Monarchs appear—impeccable, the complete aristocrats, everything the grand illusion of a departed age wished to communicate in an elegant gesture or in the disposition of a well-groomed head. Major Monarch and his wife matchlessly stand there, and the artist sketches, but the sketches fail. The sketches fail again and again until an Italian immigrant and a bright-eyed cockney named Miss Churm throw themselves into vulgar stances which ape the aristocracy. The pictures, from these models, come out marvels. The artist does not copy; he merely takes the hint, ponders his incomplete ideal, and works to fill in what is missing. The real thing of the Monarchs leaves no fertile gaps and overpowers inspiration, while Churm's "performance was simply suggestive; but it was a word to the wise" ("Real," VIII, 245). The real thing destroys the energetic application of the imagination, here artistic and aesthetic, elsewhere psychological, moral, broadly political. "When I drew the Monarchs," the artist says, "I couldn't, somehow, get away from them—get into the character I wanted to represent; and I had not the least desire my model should be discoverable in my picture. Miss Churm never was, and Mrs. Monarch thought I hid her, very properly, because she was vulgar; whereas if she was lost it was only as the dead who go to heaven are lost—in the gain of an angel the more" ("Real," VIII, 249).

That Roderick Hudson begins as something of a Hellenist and ends as a Dutch realist indicates a troubling decline, in James's aesthetic view. Such a decline approximates the temporary shift of the artist in "The Real Thing." Mrs. Monarch proudly tells him—"Now the drawings you make from *us*, they look exactly like us" ("Real," VIII, 249), little understanding how she condemns her inspiration. Finally, the artist understands "that Major and Mrs. Monarch did me permanent harm, got me into a second-rate trick" ("Real," VIII, 258). Ironically, false ways to this artist are the ways which accurately follow the real thing. The tale offers a suggestive treatment of an old theme, here secularized but in later works less secular and more complex: he who loses the world shall gain the world.

Despite considerable critical tradition, early and late in his career Henry James was a shaky realist, even when one might acknowledge the latitude any definition of realism might allow. More often than not what is *absent* provides surer vitality, and so there can be little surprise when an H. Peter Stowell complains that "for years James has been uneasily linked with the realism of Zola, Turgenev, Howells, and Twain." Stowell investigates James as an impressionist at the beginning of modernism and explores impressionism as "an ephemeral notion caught between the declarations of realism and the manifestos of expressionism, symbolism, and imagism."[21] He sensitively perceives the link between James's vision and that of Henry Adams as that of "a supersensual world, in which he [Adams] could measure nothing except by chance collisions of movements imperceptible to his sense, perhaps even imperceptible to instruments, but perceptible to each other, and so to some known ray at the end of the scale."[22] Talk of "realism" strains under too great a burden here, as does concern with perception in Henry James. The silences and imperceptibilities in the text are significant neither as clinically observed phenomena nor as occult transcendence. The real thing becomes as questionable an affair as the ghosts of Bly.

Although no important ghosts people "The Madonna of the Future" or "The Real Thing," in both tales the focus of vitality is that which is missing. Todorov concludes that several of James's tales are "based on the quest for an absolute and absent cause," and that the important issue is how to "render absence present."[23] He asserts that in these narratives an "essential secret," of something not named, is "of an absent and powerful force which sets the whole present machinery of the narrative in motion." His view, developed along structural lines, limits itself to those tales like "The Turn of the Screw" and "In the Cage," tales which develop as variations of detective fiction genres. His sense of "quest" makes such an emphasis inevitable—a sense perhaps appropriate in describing Strether's impulse in *The Ambassadors*, but less relevant to Maggie Verver's discovery or to Milly Theale's sublime adventure. Todorov acknowledges that "James's last tales avoid so categorical a formulation of any opinion whatever,"[24] and the intentions do seem to go beyond those Todorov has described. Eventually the kinesis of quest, question, and apparent action are replaced by actual withdrawal from question, quest, and overt pressure.

An extreme of morbid withdrawal develops in "The Altar of the Dead" (1895), a tale bathed, in the view of some critics, in a necrological gloom. After the death of his fiancée, George Stransom evolves a religion of the Dead, complete with the props of a blazing altar and a candle for each departed friend. In other tales the evacuated centers provide sources of passion, but here an increased perversity seems unmistakable—"He had formed little by little the habit of numbering his Dead. . . . They were there in their simplified, intensified essence, their conscious absence and expressive patience, as personally there as if they had only been stricken dumb" ("Altar," IX, 232). He shares the rare discrimination of the symbolist consciousness, but a sharper focus introduces the darkening strain.

> He knew his candles apart, up to the colour of the flame, and would still have known them had their positions all been changed. To other imaginations they might stand for other

things—that they should stand for something to be hushed before was all he desired; but he was intensely conscious of the personal note of each and of the distinguishable way it contributed to the concert. There were hours at which he almost caught himself wishing that certain of his friends would now die, that he might establish with them in this manner a connection more charming than, as it happened, it was possible to enjoy with them in life. ["Altar," IX, 242]

A monastic, quasi-Catholic fascination, suggested mildly with Theobald's madonna, here reasserts itself. John Munro has traced the subtle growth of the decadent sensibility at *fin-de-siècle*, and he relates it to a persistent association of religious musings and perverse pain.

That is the point: exquisite appreciation of pain, exquisite thrills of anguish, exquisite adoration of suffering. Here comes in a tender patronage of Catholicism: white tapers upon the high altar, an ascetic and beautiful young priest, the great gilt monstrance, the subtle-scented and mystical license, the old-world accents of the Vulgate, of the Holy Offices; the splendor of the sacred vestments. We kneel at some hour, not too early for our convenience, repeating that solemn Latin, drinking in the Gregorian tones, with plenty of modern French sonnets in memory should the sermon be dull. But join the Church! Ah, no! better to dally with enchanting mysteries, to pass from our dream of delirium to our dream of sanctity with no coarse facts to jar upon us.[25]

Stransom, the Protestant outsider in the "temple of the old persuasion" ("Altar," IX, 238), takes pleasure in his diffuse suffering. He establishes a place in "a shrine [that] had begun as a reflection of ecclesiastical pomps"—perhaps the redundancy of Saint Peter's in *Roderick Hudson's* Rome—"but the echo had ended by growing more distinct than the sound"—and in auditory metaphor Verlaine's nuance also asserts itself. The hyperattenuated symbolist consciousness finds vital interest in what seems the opposite impulse to life.

The sound now rang out, the type blazed at him with all its fires and with a mystery of radiance in which endless meanings could glow. The thing became, as he sat there, his appropriate altar, and each starry candle an appropriate vow. He numbered them, he named them, he grouped them—it was the silent roll-call of his Dead. ["Altar," IX, 239]

Yeats began *The Oxford Book of Modern Verse* with a prose piece, Walter Pater's "La Gioconda," and he called it the first modern poem. In some sense Stransom recollects Pater's description.

> . . . she is like the vampire, she had been dead many times, and learned the secrets of the grave; and has been a diver in deep seas, and keeps their fallen days about her.[26]

The vampirish Stransom makes his visits to the chapel—"these plunges were into depths quieter than the deep sea-caves" ("Altar," IX, 241)— as he explores secrets beyond the grave. Pater called "La Gioconda" the "symbol of the modern idea," and he suggested a new consciousness— tinged with darkness—when he noted "a touch of something sinister" in her. Stransom does not "burn with a hard, gemlike flame," but, on the altar of the dead, when all the candles glow together—"a brightness vast and intense, a brightness in which the mere chapel of his thoughts grew so dim" ("Altar," IX, 239)—Pater's sense is evoked. Surely Pater would have claimed that Stransom distorted his intentions; to Pater life's brevity made discrimination imperative at every moment. The antithesis of life inspires George Stransom.

Although he reveals the aesthete's distaste for positivity, Stransom's multiplied consciousness seems particularly perverse. Eventually he meets a sympathetic woman, a more forceful version of the "essentially plain" Mary Garland of *Roderick Hudson*. This unnamed woman "had no colour, no sound, no fault" ("Altar," IX, 244); she fascinates Stransom, partly because she too has built an altar, to her singular Dead. Her superiority is developed, cryptically, in relation to her wordlessness; both Stransom and the lady "forgive" the offense of Acton Hague, "but how little he had achieved the miracle that she had achieved! His forgiveness was silence, but hers was mere unuttered sound" ("Altar," IX, 261). Her more vibrant quietness fascinates him, and their rela- tionship deepens, only to enervate when he carries it further.

> After he had been with her three or four times it seemed to him that to have come at last into her house had had the horrid effect of diminishing their intimacy. He had known her better, had liked her with greater freedom, when they merely

walked together or kneeled together. Now they only pretended. . . . it was a horrible mutilation of their lives. ["Altar," IX, 262–63]

"The Altar of the Dead" presents the perversion of sensibility, the fixation on the "not there" in life and the consequent exclusion of much of human intercourse. As fascinating as Stransom appears, he devours himself in a Baudelairean obsession; viewing his altar for the last time, he cries out to his friend, " 'They say there's a gap in the array—they say it's not full, complete. Just one more,' he went on softly—'isn't that what you wanted? Yes, one more, one more.' 'Ah, no more—no more!' she wailed, as with a quick, new horror of it, under her breath." The story then ends with the grim report that Stransom's face "had the whiteness of death" ("Altar," IX, 271). The space in the altar of which Stransom speaks fills with negation; the end of his quest means annihilation. Although the force of the tale may be perverse, no ghosts materialize. Each of the Dead merely gets a candle marker and a sacred flame. After 1895, however, the "absence par excellence" of ghosts assumes more aggressive shape.

"The Friends of the Friends"[27] (1896) bridges the gap between the relatively undefined absences of the earlier tales and the complex silences of the major period. In it ghosts abound. Two people who never have met and who it seems never will meet—despite attempts by their friends to get them together—share something extraordinary. Both saw visions of a parent dying hundreds of miles away. The narrator, engaged to the mysterious gentleman, for many years attempts to get the two together. Finally, on the night of her sudden death, the ghostly lady enters the gentleman's room and finally they do meet. The story attempts to determine, through comparisons of watches and clocks, and through testimonies of drowsy charwomen and shiftless porters, if the lady appeared to the gentleman just *before* or just *after* she dropped gently dead. Had she been alive or had she been dead? As the tale develops it becomes clear that, because the two do not meet, because the rendezvous remains eternally absent, feelings grow enormously between them. Never can they get together—"A cold, a headache, a bereavement, a storm, a fog, an earthquake, a cataclysm infallibly intervened. The whole business was beyond a joke."

Yet as a joke it had still to be taken, though one couldn't help feeling that the joke made the situation serious, had produced on the part of each consciousness, an awkwardness, a positive dread of the last accident of all, the only one with any freshness left, the accident that would bring them face to face. ["Friends," IX, 378]

"The Friends of the Friends" is important because it deals, in simplified and sensationalized terms, with the patterns of *The Wings of the Dove*. As Dorothea Krook has noted, the situation in the two works is almost identical—"that of a man falling in love with the memory of a dead woman, as a quasi-supernatural phenomenon in the tale, as perfectly naturalistic (if not wholly natural) in the novel."[28] Near the end of each, a distressed heroine realizes that her fiancé is in love with a dead girl. In "The Friends of the Friends," but also in the story of Milly Theale, a man loves a woman who, to him, has always been a near-absent, silent presence. Neither tale presents ordinary love or ordinary mourning for a vital creature whose life was snuffed out. The mourning seems morbid, at least to some readers and to the women who lose their lovers.

> "I'm life, you see," I answered. "What you saw last night was death."
> "It was life—it was life!" . . . "Oh, *she* was alive! she was, she was!"
> "She was dead! she was dead!" I asserverated with an energy, a determination that it should *be* so, which comes back to me now as grotesque. But the sound of the word as it rang out filled me suddenly with sudden horror. ["Friends," IX, 393–94]

Comparisons of watches and sleepy testimonies are beside the point here, for a deeper modernist question is being argued over, and in some ways the debate concerns the symbolist consciousness. Some people will assert that the silences are silences, that absences are absences, gaps merely empty stretches, and that attempts to make them the stuff of life are morbid attempts. "They're dead, they're dead," one faction claims, and "How they live!" the other calls back. It is a matter of a hair; five minutes in the wrong direction and the woman is dead, but get the clock on the wall, at the right moment, at the right angle, and the woman was, gloriously enough, alive. The issue remains ambiguous, and although throughout much of his career James asserts the integrity of motivating silences, the "absolute and absent cause" of Todorov's criticism, at points such as these the questions balance on a brink. The passion that comes in the tale reveals itself only through gestures which seem the negations of passion.

"In the Cage" was written in 1898, the same year as "The Turn of the Screw," but in it no ordinary ghosts appear. An unnamed telegraph clerk holds copies of three cryptic telegrams that involve Captain Everard and Lady Bradeen. From these fragmented words, the young clerk develops a complex and impassioned story concerning these vaguely romantic people. "In the Cage" presents over a hundred pages of a young woman's attempts to read life where no definite life exists, and, at the moment of epiphany, her thoughts are presented in characteristic terms—"Then it was that, above all, she felt how much she had missed in the gaps and blanks and absent answers—how much she had to dispense with" ("Cage," X, 220). Here she realizes the error in reading the words she transcribes, rather than the silences between them and gauging their tensions.

Romantic poetry was resonant with the implication of voice, but, as Clive Scott has asserted, in modernistic expression "the theoretical rhetorical punctuation of a line is translated into sounded silence, the reverberations of exclamation, the expiration of despair, the baffled silence of question." Scott indicates how Mallarmé was among the first to appreciate "the poetic responsibility that can be born by blank space."[29] Like the woman in the cage, Mallarmé felt that:

> L'armature intellectuelle du poème se dissimule et tient— a lieu—dans l'espace qui isole les strophes et parmi le blanc du papier: signicatif silence qu'il n'est pas moins beau de composer que les vers. ["The intellectual substructure of the poem conceals itself, is present—is active—in the blank space which separates the stanzas and in the white of the paper: a pregnant silence, no less wonderful to compose than the lines themselves."][30]

Here James's story of an unromantic heroine offers expression of the theory that blank space held "the utter virtuality of thought": "Penser étant écrire sans accessoires, ni chuchotement mais tacite encore l'immortelle parole" ["To think being to write without accessories or whispering, but with the immortal word still implicit"],[31] an expression of Mallarmé's Crise de vers. The tale comes close to the bone of such a quasi-linguistic theme, but it can claim only moderate success and never attains the luminosity which Mallarmé sought. The trapped, the petty, the slightly less-than-human hold up in the cage, and the essence of childish cryptography rather than more subtle symbolist divination carries the heroine to her questionable end.

Yet it is interesting to note that "In the Cage" resembles the story of the governess at Bly. Two unnamed young women from deprived backgrounds find themselves caged-up as observers of implied grand sin. Both get a few clues and both construct portentous plots. In "The Turn of the Screw" it may be that the more developed modernist consciousness reads legitimate evanescences in the air—call them ghosts, metaphoric or literal—but eventually a decadent awareness, restless and hypersensible, stalks the various nuances of darkness, negation, and moral perversity. The governess works for an exorcism of demons, but the tale ends with an extreme chill. With "In the Cage" the pulsing absences seem less threatening, as does the imagination which works upon them; and what is questionably imagined at Bly is definitely imagined in the second tale.

Gone is the arch pressure of the governess's silence, a charged silence perhaps not entirely unlike the manipulative wordlessness with which, in *The Golden Bowl*, Maggie Verver will make Charlotte Stant do her will. Here a young woman believes herself an important character in the life of an aristocratic gentleman whose messages she transmits. When he comes into her office, desperate to retrieve an incriminating telegram, he tells her, "It wasn't delivered, you see. We've got to recover it." She is "struck with the beauty of his plural pronoun" ("Cage," X, 221–22), his including her in on his problem. Yet the "we" more likely refers to him and his panicking paramour.

A girl who "was perfectly aware that her imaginative life was the life in which she spent most of her time" ("Cage," X, 143), she resents, too, the marriage proposal of Mr. Mudge, and indeed she resents too much "presence" intruding on her more significant imaginative life— "The only weakness in her faculty came from the positive abundance of her contact with the human herd; this was so constant, had the effect of becoming so cheap, that there were long stretches in which inspiration, divination and interest, quite dropped" ("Cage," X, 143). Because she knows so little about Captain Everard, she falls in love with him. His words mean little to her compared to his silences—"His words were mere numbers, they told her nothing whatever; and after he had gone she was in possession of no name, of no address, of no meaning, of nothing but a vague, sweet sound and an immense impression" ("Cage," X, 148). Again, in *The Golden Bowl*, sound will become silence and silence sound, most impressively perhaps when Charlotte's forced muteness rings out to Maggie as the wail of a tormented animal.

Timid in the face of presences, the telegram clerk dislikes patrons about whom she knows more than very little—"They're *too* real!" she says, and then dismisses them as "horrid" ("Cage," X, 164). Silence, or near silence, becomes the goal and the tribute in this slightly pathetic comic tale.

> But she forebore as yet to speak; she had not spoken even to Mrs. Jordan; and the hush that on her lips surrounded the Captain's name maintained itself as a kind of symbol of the success that, up to this time, had attended something or other— she couldn't have said what—that she humoured herself with calling, without words, her relation with him. ["Cage," X, 172]

Then the gentleman enters and tips his hat, and she says that she hasn't seen him in ages. He replies, "Oh, yes, hasn't it been awfully wet?"

> That was a specimen of their give and take; it fed her fancy that no form of intercourse so transcendent and distilled had ever been established on earth. Everything, so far as they chose to consider it so, might mean almost anything. . . . It may be imagined, therefore, how their unuttered reference to all she knew about him could, in this immensity, play at its ease. ["Cage," X, 173]

It borders on light-hearted madness; nonetheless, the telegrammatic lady is as ravenous for unspoken clues as the governess of "The Turn of the Screw." When Lady Bradeen finally appears, the clerk stares at her lips—"looked at them with a strange passion that, for an instant, had the result of filling out some of the gaps, supplying the missing answers, in his correspondence. . . . She was with the absent through her ladyship and with her ladyship through the absent" ("Cage," X, 180).

But here at least no little boy dies at the end. When she finally meets the captain outside on the street, what she conceives as a grand drama is probably, to him, a passing encounter with a modified shopgirl. She builds on virtually nothing—but she reads pulses in that nothingness. He is polite, but a blank canvas—"at this point, by mere action of his silence, everything they had so definitely not named, the whole presence round which they had been circling, became a part of their reference, settled solidly between them" ("Cage," X, 198). When they meet again, the silence means more to her—"nothing passed between them but the fulness of their silence" ("Cage," X, 208). On tip-toe of romantic exhilaration, she thinks this polite but disinterested young man is half in love with her, or perhaps more than half.

This sensitive young woman lives with her ghosts within, but they are as veritable hallucinations as ever stalked a manor house. The "reality" of the ghost of "The Turn of the Screw" seems increasingly doubtful when we consider that "In the Cage" was written at almost the same time. The attention which has gone to "The Turn of the Screw" is fascinating but similar questions could be asked concerning many other works. Is life that is lived for silent, ghostly forces, for solidifying or abstracted symbolist silences, life at all, or is it foolish, fictive, comic, morbid? Finally the clerk decides it has not been worth all that much; she gathers plenty of details about Everard and turns away from the false dream of the absent to accept Mr. Mudge's proposal for a life of homey groceries, cabbage, stuck-in-the-mud plenitudes. She decides that "her little home must be not for next month, but for next week" ("Cage," X, 242), and she leaves the cage—the title seems ironic indeed—of the imagination. The reader may cheer her on, mildly, this woman who finally chooses the real thing, but her position is not that of later heroines. The nameless, faceless clerk who works her machine in proximity to the smell of vegetables shows an imaginative spark, but she betrays an undisciplined awareness of the serious silences she reads. She has her minor heroisms, but she remains insignificant. She is better off married to Mr. Mudge, with his Dickensian name and his undoubtedly ruddy arms.

The Dickensian reference is not gratuitous. An aesthetic movement which nurtured oversubtilized impulses in exotic capitals was worlds away from the caricatured vitality of Mayfair shopkeeps. Attributing hypersensitivity to a creature who punched a time-clock would have seemed foolishness to The Yellow Book crowd. Whistler's peacocks might share few vibrations with a woman called both "magpie" and "guinea-pig," and the sweet fragrance of near-decay would have little to do with "the presence of hams, cheese, dried fish, soap, varnish, paraffins and

other solids and fluids that she came to know perfectly by their smells."
It is no wonder that the anonymous telegraphic lady chooses a small
degree of positivity with a husband. Attenuated sensibilities and awareness of an ambiguously negative universe best belong to the rich, the
great, the glutted—even if they are glutted by the subtleties of Schubert
and Scarlatti, Titian and Fra Angelico, absinthe and liquor Monacho-
rum Benedictinorum Abbatie Fiscanensis. The *via negativa* toward fulfillment may suit best those who can give up most. The positivistic
and apparently healthy turn at the end of "In the Cage," into marriage,
home, and family, is therefore—and critically—more of a renunciation
than at first it may seem. The young woman chooses to leave her ghosts
behind, but they remain worthy presences, and they soon regain considerable force—at the same time more promising and more shadowy.

In "Maud-Evelyn" (1900) Marmaduke, a young traveler in Switzer-
land, meets the parents of a girl who died young, but whose memory
they have kept alive to such an extent that they have begun to amend
the facts of her life. Although she barely reached adolescence, they
have begun to talk of her as having been older and older, as having
had many beaux, and as, almost, having made a marriage. At first
fascinated by their twisted and intense love, Marmaduke soon begins
to be taken in by their fantasy. Eventually he believes that Maud-
Evelyn and he had contact and one day they married. Once the parents,
the Dedricks, get their daughter "married off," they expire in a gentle
way, these forty-year-old "old people," and they leave everything to
Marmaduke. Soon Marmaduke reports that his wife, Maud-Evelyn, has
"died," and then soon after he enfeebles and dies himself, leaving the
Dedrick riches to the woman he had proposed to before he "met" Maud-
Evelyn.

This strange story works an imaginative embroidery similar to that
of "In the Cage," but here the effect, in Leon Edel's words, is a "venture
into morbidity,"[32] an excursion with none of the comedy or relief of
the melodramatic telegraphic clerk's story. Like that clerk, Marmaduke
begins pale and rather lifeless; he gets lugged to Europe by a maiden
aunt, begins to take in tidbits of information about the Dedrick girl,
and then on his own he fabricates, rather energetically, many details.
The process invigorates him, and when he tells the narrator about the
gifts he "made" to Maud-Evelyn, he exhibits more spirit than he ever
had before.

"Those I made her. She loved each one, and I remember about each the particular thing she said. Though I do say it," he continued, "none of the others, as a matter of fact, come near mine. I look at them every day, and I assure you I'm not ashamed." Evidently, in short, he had spared nothing, and he talked on and on. He really quite swaggered. ["Maud," XI, 69]

It is because of this "affair" with the eternally absent Maud-Evelyn that the narrator and her friend Lavinia, Marmaduke's first intended, decide that "He had had his life," and had had "his sum of passion . . . spent" ("Maud," XI, 73).

Yet there is something disturbing *en famille* about the marriage between Marmaduke and Maud-Evelyn. Marmaduke admits, "It's as ridiculous as you please, but they've simply adopted me" ("Maud,", XI, 57), and he grows fat in the role and "might perfectly have passed for the handsome, happy, full-blown son of doting parents who couldn't let him out of view" ("Maud," XI, 60). He spends so much time in the role of son that when he weds Maud-Evelyn, whom the reader has come to accept as his sister, morbidity compounds with the hint of incest or at least an increasing inversion of imaginative function. Something of the House of Usher informs the story of Marmaduke and Maud-Evelyn: everything turns inward, dessicates, wastes away, and withers. James explores the egotistical and morbid potential of the imaginative mind which is drawn to absences, blanks, the dead and departed or the barely born. In Poe's story the house tears asunder, but the more genteel pessimism of Henry James leaves the set strewn with gently expiring gentlepeople.

Egotism is a major concern in the fiction. The egotism of Isabel Archer, as well as that of her husband, is linked to enervation at least as early as *The Portrait of a Lady*. The imaginative talent, so attractive in the Albany heiress and in her fictive descendants, is constantly ambiguous. Imagination gives "life" where life is not, and some will argue that such life is really a face of death, as dead as the girl in "Maud-Evelyn," and just as unreal. In one way or another James's imaginative characters build an altar of the dead, the unborn, the ghostly, the absent. Isabel Archer marries a man who, by her own admission, is a complete nonentity; her action is a characteristic but nonetheless fatal mistake of an exceptionally imaginative Jamesian. Almost twenty years after the publication of *The Portrait of a Lady* another imaginative character weds himself to a clinical nonentity, someone blanker than Osmond, someone even deader, if less malevolent, than Osmond. Like Isabel, Marmaduke chooses the barely-there over the flesh and blood lover, over the woman the narrator defends with her cry, "Live for *my* girl. Live for Lavinia" ("Maud," XI, 52).

In his study of James and the requirements of the imagination, Philip M. Weinstein presents illuminating discussions of imagination that is artistic, exploitative, passionate, vicarious, appreciative, moral, fastidious, and, finally, failed. Weinstein's sense of failed imagination is one we might associate with the imagination, or lack of imagination, of the Pococks of Woollett, of Mrs. Newsome stiffly sitting up back home, or of those people completely immune to Marie de Vionnet's infinite variety.[33] But James also presents failure when an imagination is too active, too all-encompassing. Quentin Anderson is perhaps right to say that "James is truer than William Blake to a vision of the world as wholly the product of the human imagination,"[34] but there are strong suggestions, as early as 1881 and right up through the late novels and tales, that imagination can fall into decadence when it takes for its own all the kingdoms of the earth.

"The Jolly Corner," in Todorov's view the densest of James's short stories,[35] was published in 1908, four years after *The Golden Bowl*. Spencer Brydon returns to America after 33 years abroad and, in New York, begins to explore a vacant house he owns and would have lived in had he not shifted to Europe. His preoccupation, soon to become an obsession, is with the question of *who* he might have become had he remained in America. He roams the house for this absent other self and eventually he sees it, is terrified, and rejects it. Like John Marcher, Brydon has tremendous imaginative interest in seemingly empty places. "The Beast in the Jungle," however, may be less of a success because in it the void holds little energy; John Marcher waits before a dull and dusty affair. Undergraduates moan that nothing happens. In this one tale almost nothing *does* happen in all the quietus—except for the shock at the end, and consequently not all readers can comprehend John Marcher's fascination.

In "The Jolly Corner" James seems to re-treat relevant concerns, and he uses similar imagery throughout. Strongly reminiscent of the earlier tale, the narration of "The Jolly Corner" reports that Brydon "had tasted no pleasure so fine as his actual tension, had been introduced to no sport that demanded at once the patience and the nerve of this stalking of a creature more subtle, yet at bay perhaps more formidable, than any beast of the forest" ("Jolly," XII, 210). Unlike those in John

Marcher's tale, however, the absences of "The Jolly Corner" are active places. As Martha Banta writes of Brydon, "In his rush after the unseen, only imagined presence fleeing before him through the blank rooms, he experiences, as never before, the thrill and flush of real life."[36] Here the voids are charged and, when Brydon shows Alice Staverton the house, "while they walked through the great blank rooms, the absolute vacancy reigned" ("Jolly," XII, 199). Ghosts, it would seem, are inevitable. Even the city of New York, the Babylon of heroic materialism, lives in terms of its absences.

> It seemed to him he had waited an age for some stir of the great grim hush; the life of the town was itself under a spell—so unnaturally, up and down the whole prospect of known and rather ugly objects, the blankness and silence lasted. . . . Great builded voids, great crowded stillnesses put on, often, in the heart of the cities, for the small hours, a sort of sinister mask, and it was of this large collective negation that Brydon presently became conscious. ["Jolly," XII, 220–21]

The *large collective negation*—negation indoors, negation out, negation of his own history—becomes the fertile field of Brydon's search. Indeed, collective negation increasingly develops as the atmosphere of consciousness for James's characters. At moments it seems to lead to madness.

Elizabeth Stevenson has noted that "Keats's relation to the world of the senses, the intense awareness which he had of other presences, was similar to James'."[37] Keats and James did have much in common, but perhaps their sense of negation was crucially different. The extreme of what Keats saw as the "negative capability" of the poetic character

> . . . is not itself—it has no self—it is every thing and nothing—it has no character—it enjoys light and shade. . . . A Poet is the most unpoetical of any thing in existence; because he has no Identity—he is continually in for—and filling some other Body—The Sun, the Moon, the Sea and Men and Women who are creatures of impulse. . . . When I am in a room with People if I ever am free from speculating on creations of my own brain, then not myself goes home to myself: but the identity of every one in the room begins to press upon me that I am in a very little time annihilated.[38]

Annihiliation is what Spencer Brydon also risks—but the threat seems more serious. His sense of life becomes sufficiently divorced from self—although for a time he believes this alter ego is self—that he nearly gives up self entirely. Although he seems to think that this "other" world mirrors, invigorates, and deepens his own life, when he meets its sole inhabitant face-to-face, Brydon feels a "falling back as under the hot breath and roused passion of a life larger than his own, a rage of personality before which his own collapsed, he felt the whole vision turn to darkness and his very feet give way" ("Jolly," XII, 226). He falls into a faint so profound that when Alice Staverton finds him, she "had for a long unspeakable moment not doubted he was dead" ("Jolly," XII, 228). The Jamesian hero comes close to oblivion, but this is not Keats, for the annihilation is darker. This man is not subsumed by the "Sun, the Moon, the Sea and Men and Women," but by "blankness and stillness," by "absolute vacancy," by "great builded voids." Spencer Brydon is not near-annihilated by life, but rather by the ghostly creation which his own imagination places in the void.

"Negative capability" and the "collective negation" of Henry James move in different directions. Keats was perhaps most of all excited by the presences of life, the juicy syrops, the dark eyes of a mistress, the marks of autumn. His "still unravished bride of quietness/ Thou foster child of silence" is born of physicality, of actualization in life, of the earth, of the forest branches and the trodden weed. The romantic poet reacted to something far different than the symbolist silences. Responding to Keats's letter on negative capability, Hazlitt spoke of Shakespeare as "the least of an egotist that it was possible to be. He was nothing in himself; but he was all the others were, or that they could become."[39] Such is little like the character of James's hero, and, as in "Maud-Evelyn," uneasy inversion recurs again and again. With Isabel Archer, with Marmaduke, and with Spencer Brydon, the exciting "other" has little or no Keatsian integrity, but rather "other" provides a metaphoric emptiness into which an aspect of self may be projected. Necessarily distorted, sometimes monstrous, it asserts itself as something before which "real" life pales.

The Jamesian negative capability holds the potential for developing an immense and withering egotism. The morbidly sensitive eye rakes the boulevard and then inevitably turns inward. Symons wrote that the characteristic decadent is "partly the father, partly the offspring of the perverse art that he adores,"[40] and such an extreme develops in "The Jolly Corner." Morbidly subtle intensity gives birth to a new self, for Brydon is both father and son, subject and object of his own ego-tistical fascination. The old heaven and earth are lost, and the reality that signifies shrinks to the focus of the self-reflecting mind. A modern intelligence abandons the spirits of other ages, and the result may seem frightening. Hannah Arendt has said that secular man, "modern man at any rate, did not gain life, strictly speaking, either; he was thrust back upon it, thrown into the closed inwardness of introspection, where the highest he could experience were empty processes of reckoning of the mind, its play with itself."[41] The eternally absent other emphatically becomes one with self, and the fiction moves onto an arid plain of isolation. Aestheticism, eccentricity, and exquisite modern sensibility refine imagination until it goes too far and moves against the grain, leaving its masters sometimes as effete, epicene, and pale as Des Esseintes or the Marquis d'O, vitiations of exhausted races.

When near the end of The Portrait of a Lady Isabel Archer sees the ghost of Gardencourt, she views an ill-defined but complex creature with many ancestors and more descendants. It appears again and again in James, each time ambiguously hovering, prompting the question of whether or not the extreme imaginative life is empty or full, the way of damnation or of grace. The ghost means all these things and more, and it is really half-dead and half-alive at the same time, as are all ghosts. In the tales, absence par excellence more often than not leads to darkness and failure, but, in the developed work of the later novels, more subtle silences reassert themselves as positive concerns of vital experience.

4 Dialectical Marriages: *The Portrait of a Lady* and *The Spoils of Poynton*

> *"If there were more there would be too many to convey the impression in which half the beauty resides—the impression, somehow, of something dreamed and missed, something reduced, relinquished, resigned: the poetry, as it were, of something sensibly gone."*
>
> Fleda Vetch in *The Spoils of Poynton*

In *The Portrait of a Lady* a young woman from upstate New York stands in the doorway of a magnificent English country house. With brimming anticipation she surveys the great lawn before her, and then, as the gentlemen in the distance look up and stare, startled over their teacups, she moves toward them. Isabel Archer enters as one of the most vibrant women in American fiction, and she is the finest young woman these perceptive gentlemen have ever seen. Then she marries Gilbert Osmond. An attractive American who might have fared well with either of two handsome millionaires chooses the man her friends refer to as the quietest man in Europe, someone essentially defined by what he lacks, by the silences that show him or do not show him to the world. When Madame Merle first describes him to Isabel, she says, "He is Gilbert Osmond—he lives in Italy; that is all one can say about him. He is exceedingly clever, a man made to be distinguished; but, as I say, you exhaust the description when you say he is Mr. Osmond, who lives in Italy. No career, no name, no position, no fortune, no past, no future, no anything."[1] Isabel's fascination grows and persists, and later, when Caspar Goodwood pleads with her, she declares, "Give me up, Mr. Goodwood; I am marrying a nonentity. Don't try to take an interest in him; you can't" (p. 289).

The scene where Gilbert Osmond encircles his ankle with thumb and forefinger evokes the unmistakable chill of the decadents. In 1885, four years after the publication of *Portrait*, J. K. Huysmans examined similar over-refinement in "the Duc Jean des Esseintes, a frail young man of thirty, anaemic and nervous, with hollow cheeks, eyes of a cold, steely blue, a small but still straight nose, and long, slender hands."

> By a curious accident of heredity, this last scion of a race bore a strong resemblance to the far-off ancestor, the mignon of Princes, from whom he had got the pointed beard of the very palest possible blond and expression, which marked the portrait.[2]

In 1881 Osmond himself had

> a thin, delicate, sharply-cut face, of which the only fault was that it looked too pointed; an appearance to which the shape of the beard contributed not a little. This beard, cut in the manner of the portraits of the sixteenth century and sur-mounted by a fair moustache, of which the ends had a pic-turesque upward flourish, gave its wearer a somewhat foreign traditionary look, and suggested that he was a gentleman who studied effect. His luminous intelligent eye [was] an eye which expressed both softness and keenness. . . . [p. 199]

Languid but energetic, vague but penetrating, these two men represent the perverse fusion of opposites which intrigued the 1880s. Both are notable connoisseurs of specimens, Des Esseintes in a monastic chateau filled with tongueless orchids, Osmond in a forbidding villa—"it looked somehow as if, once you were in, it would not be easy to get out" (p. 221)—with magnifying glass and miniature watercolor brush. Both have ungodly religious obsessions, Osmond simply desiring to be Pope, Des Esseintes complexly yearning for "the aroma of the Church, incense, myrrh and that strange Thymiama mentioned in the Bible."[3] Both hint at peculiar sexuality. On the Rue de Rivoli Des Esseintes slackens his pace when a young man passes; Osmond gently lays his hand on Good-wood's knee and, with subtle obscenity, speaks of his marriage: "We are as united, you know, as the candlestick and the snuffers" (p. 442).

Oversubtilized and mannered and seemingly perverse, the two men share much, but Osmond claims none of the inevitable humanity of Des Esseintes, perhaps simply because Osmond does not seem to suffer. Osmond may provide James's comment, in 1881, on the decadents—

empty, perhaps hideous, yet strongly attractive, at least to certain special people. But as heiress of a symbolist age Isabel Archer is not so different from her decadent husband; she exercises a modern sensibility to make serious mistakes, causing herself to be deceived by the brilliance of Madame Merle and by Osmond's specious seductiveness. Yet traditional views exaggerate the deception; Madame Merle does little more than describe Osmond in terms already noted, in distinctly negated terms as persistent "absence par excellence," and then she choreographs the meeting of the two singular youngish people. Her motives may be deceptive, but her plan is straightforward. Isabel Archer sees Osmond accurately as the tasteful nonentity she chooses over a pair of eminently positivistic suitors. Her choice reflects her character and the character of others at the century's end.

Many forces work to transform the overwhelmingly anti-materialistic bias of Isabel Archer, but the money and the travel change little. Ralph Touchett may give her absolute potential for plenitude, in the shape of a mountain of money, and an aunt may hand over the wide world, but Isabel poor and Isabel rich share the same fascinations and they err in similar ways. With an imagination that amazes everyone, she prefers a life that is more exciting for what it lacks than for what it possesses. She hangs before blank walls which only for a time seem portals to a richer life. Her imagination stirs in the quiet and there she finds the expression which best suits her.

When her aunt descends upon Albany, Isabel is firmly set in the position she long will maintain and will only understand when she finds her life with Osmond "a dark, narrow alley, with a dead wall at the end" (p. 371). Somewhat like Milly Theale turning her face to the wall, Isabel, however, does not attain the victory of the later heroine. Isabel's is a sitting stance, more preoccupied with what exists behind metaphoric silences than with actualities of engaged experience. Mrs. Touchett first finds her in a mysterious apartment:

> The place owed much of its mysterious melancholy to the fact that it was properly entered from the second door of the house, the door that had been condemned, and that was fastened by bolts which a particularly slender little girl found it impossible to slide. She knew that this silent, motionless portal opened into the street; if the sidelights had not been filled with green paper, she might have looked out upon the little brown stoop and the well-worn brick pavement. But she

> had no wish to look out, for this would have interfered with her theory that there was a strange, unseen place on the other side—a place which became, to the child's imagination, according to its different moods, a region of delight or of terror. [p. 19]

In time she engages herself to Gilbert Osmond, a man who approximates the suggestiveness of that portal; indeed at first he—or his house—is considered in terms of similarly vacant architectural features.

> The villa was a long rather blank-looking structure. . . . It was the mask of the house; it was not its face. It had heavy lids, but no eyes. . . . The windows of the ground-floor, as you saw them from the piazza, were, in their noble proportions, extremely architectural; but their function seemed less to offer communication with the world than to defy the world to look in. [pp. 197–98]

The Albany house in which Isabel Archer at first sits is hardly more inviting than Osmond's—"At this time she might have had the whole house to choose from, and the room she had selected was the most joyless chamber it contained. She had never opened the bolted door nor removed the green paper (renewed by other hands) from its sidelights; she had never assured herself that the vulgar street lay beyond it" (p. 19). In the New York Edition of 1908, when Osmond declares his wish to marry Isabel, an intensified image fuses the New York portal with the attraction of her hyper-elegant suitor. The childhood bolts finally move—"The tears came into her eyes; this time they obeyed the sharpness of the pang that suggested to her somehow the slipping of a fine bolt—backward, forward, she couldn't have said which."[4] The bolts slip forward and, as in Albany, Isabel faces a wall, although she does not yet know it. The marriage of Gilbert Osmond to Isabel Archer is not the sleight-of-hand some readers consider it.

Anticipating the symbolists, Baudelaire wrote with full praise of the habit of mind which an Isabel Archer demonstrates. In *Les Fenêtres* he enlarged upon the proposition that imagination best thrives behind subtle barriers which invest the common and the hidden with unsuspected life.

Celui qui regard du dehors à travers une fenêtre ouverte, ne voit jamais autant de choses que celui qui regard une fenêtre fermée. Il n'est pas d'objet plus profond, plus mystérieux, plus fécond, plus ténébreux, plus éblouissant qu'une fenêtre éclairée d'une chandelle. . . . ["Looking through an open window from the outside you never see as much as when you look at a shut window. Nothing exists more profound, more mysterious, more creative, more shadowy, or more dazzling. . . . "][5]

Watching before the closed door in Albany, Isabel Archer approaches the consciousness of the developed movement of the eighties. Like the twilight chambers in the paintings which Goldwater examines, those of Redon, Ensor, Carrière, Khnopff, and Klinger, Isabel's retreated office, existing in an "indeterminate space, only partially emerging from the surrounding darkness, contains the suggestion of the mysterious reality beyond appearance that is proper to symbolism."[6] As surely as is the case with these modernist painters, the initial image of Isabel Archer, "which stresses a concentration upon the unseen and unheard, and in its handling, which suggests more than it depicts, is character- istic" of the movement of symbolism at its inception.[7]

Critics have suggested James's debt to Baudelaire, not for joyless carnality, to be sure, but for the fascinating scent of evil inside the drawing room. Yet James may also have learned something from Bau- delaire's alienating modernist landscape, an urban field in demise which sends the poetic imagination back onto itself.

Multitude, solitude: terme égaux et convertibles pour le poète actif et fécond. Qui ne sait pas peupler sa solitude, ne sait pas non plus être seul dans une foule affairée. [Multitude, solitude: equivalent and interchangeable terms to the shaping spirit of the poet. If you don't know how to people your solitude, you don't know either how to be alone in a busy crowd.][8]

Isabel Archer prefers Baudelaire's withdrawn but fecond isolation. Her habit links her to other hermetic sensibilities—Osmond's and Des Esseintes's among them—that prefer the ironic positivity of a negative life that is cloistered, or imprisoned, depending upon the sympathy or severity of the outsider's judgment.

Another Jamesian fascinated with the force of silences which seem dead to others, Isabel possesses an imagination which is described as "ridiculously active" (p. 26). Only an extraordinary imagination might fall in love with Osmond's unblemished canvas of cool presence and invest it with life. Isabel, whom Osmond considers "the most imaginative woman he had known" (p. 373), seems equal to that difficult task. "It might very well have been true; for during those months she had imagined a world of things that had no substance. She had a vision of him—she had not read him right. A certain combination of features had touched her, and in them she had seen the most striking of portraits" (p. 373). *The Portrait of a Lady* examines the problem of "In the Cage" and "The Real Thing," treated in a broader reference than that of a shopkeeper's workplace or an artist's atelier.

Isabel in fact values her husband for reasons similar to those for which he values his daughter. Isabel found Pansy "a sheet of blank paper" (p. 243), "a blank page, a pure white surface" (p. 276), and yet—consequently, it would seem—"the ideal *jeune fille* of foreign fiction" (p. 243). Osmond himself, Isabel tells her cousin, is defined by a similar vacancy, with "no property, no honours, no houses, no lands, no position, no reputation, no brilliant belongings of any sort. It is the total absence of all these things that pleases me" (p. 304). She chooses union with a husband who is a perfect nonentity, and as Pansy is the ideal *jeune fille*, her father appears to Isabel "the first gentleman in Europe" (p. 376).

On a small scale, Pansy provides a structural model for her father, and she claims the peculiar charm of the Osmond line, a charm Gilbert has exercised successfully at least twice, with the finest of women. It is said that Pansy will make the most splendid match, and the reader believes that she might. Isabel eventually comprehends the part the undefined daughter has played on the exercise of her stepmother's imagination.

> It seemed to show her how far her husband's desire to be effective was capable of going—to the point of playing picturesque tricks upon the delicate organism of his daughter. She could not understand his purpose, no—not wholly; but she understood it better than he supposed or desired, inasmuch as she was convinced that the whole proceeding was an elaborate mystification, addressed to herself and destined to act upon her imagination. [p. 467]

Pansy's structural silences provide sufficient nourishment to entrap, innocently, the imagination of Ned Rosier, a collector of exquisite enamels. Osmond works on a grander scale when he wins Isabel's affection—"she was deluded, but she was consistent. It was wonderfully characteristic of her that she had invented a fine theory about Gilbert Osmond, and loved him, not for what he really possessed, but for his very poverties" (p. 305). In James imaginative people repeatedly confront the real thing and choose to reject it—to wait, to watch, to maintain impatient patience, to invert themselves and dedicate themselves to the blank canvas as in "The Madonna of the Future," to spend their lives staring expectantly into the void, as in "The Beast in the Jungle," to wed themselves to a blank nonentity, as in *The Portrait of a Lady*. Lord Warburton offers Isabel overwhelming social plenitude and Caspar Goodwood promises tremendous physical reality; Osmond offers nothing tangible, and that is his powerful charm.

Isabel finally perceives that Osmond wanted her as an extension of himself—"Her mind was to be his—attached to his own like a small garden-plot to a deer park. He would rake the soil gently and water the flowers; he would weed the bed and gather an occasional nosegay" (p. 378). And yet Isabel married a man who, she thought, would have hardly more physical or spiritual independence from her, a man she loved for what he lacked—she loved him "a good deal also for what she brought him. As she looked back at the passion of those weeks she perceived in it a kind of maternal strain—the happiness of a woman who felt that she was the contributor, that she came with full hands" (p. 373). The uneasy maternal charge in this marriage, the love of a woman for something of her own creation, links Isabel Archer to the egotism of Spencer Brydon in "The Jolly Corner" and to the decadent inversion of her husband.

Positive becomes negative and negative positive in this ironical novel, and the marriage Isabel makes has its perversities. In Albany, Isabel already betrays some related confusion when she makes her declaration of her odd sense of life. Mrs. Touchett interrupts the girl at her reading and says she will sell the family house, but Isabel protests, to her aunt's dismay.

> "I don't see what makes you so fond of it; your father died here."
> "Yes; but I don't dislike it for that," said the girl, rather strangely. "I like places in which things have happened—even

if they are sad things. A great many people have died here;
the place has been full of life."
"Is that what you call being full of life?" [p. 22]

The usually short-sighted Mrs. Touchett senses the oddity of her niece's
response. A habit of reading fulness in what others find essentially
empty, or in this case dead, is part of Isabel Archer's idiosyncratic
vision and perhaps may be the heritage of Baudelairean morbidity. It
goes too far. When she meets Osmond and he reports that his most
simple plan has been all along "to be as quiet as possible," Isabel's
interest intensifies.

"Do you call that simple?" Isabel asked, with a gentle laugh.
"Yes, because it's negative."
"Has your life been negative?"
"Call it affirmative if you like." [p. 231]

She calls it affirmative. She marries him. Only later does Isabel understand the ambiguous power he will direct against her. Her aunt warns
against the marriage—"there is nothing of him," she tells Isabel, but
Isabel responds, "Then he can't hurt me" (p. 292).

The intelligent discrimination of positive from negative tests many
imaginations in James's fiction. The confusions are inevitable. Confusion, or delicate fusion, of the two seeming opposites informed the
poetics of the 1857 Les Fleurs du Mal, where Baudelaire announced "je
cherche le vide, et le noir, et le nu!" [I seek the empty, the black, the
bare], in his quest for strange new life. Consistently, as extreme symbolist consciousnesses withdrew from the corruption of materialism,
some moved from rich promise to various darknesses; it is characteristic
that Isabel Archer announces richness in a chamber not only of emptiness but of death, of multitudinous death. Criticism comments on
the chill and frigidity of the Albany heiress, but such subtle affinities—
horrific even to a dragon of an aunt—indicate a condition more dangerous than a young woman's distrust of forceful men. The vector of
Isabel Archer is not only away from vitality but towards something
contrary to vitality, inevitably as ghastly as the young man's attraction
to the vacancy of the absent Maud-Evelyn.

A disturbed consciousness rejects the superabundance of Lord Warburton, a man who is nearly a personal equivalent of Rome's splendor.
Rarely in James is anyone described in such heaping positivistic terms.

He has everything. He is everything. Mr. Touchett tells Isabel, "Lord Warburton is a very amiable young man—a very fine young man."

> He has a hundred thousand a year. He owns fifty thousand acres of the soil of this little island. He has half-a-dozen houses to live in. He has a seat in Parliament as I have one at my own dinner-table. He has very cultivated tastes—cares for literature, for art, for science, for charming young ladies. [pp. 62–63]

Mr. Touchett goes on to extend the Englishman's qualities and possessions, but Isabel comprehends that union with the gentleman would doom her fundamentally imaginative spirit. When she rejects his offer of marriage, she betrays a "coldness [which] was not coquetry—a quality that she possessed in much smaller degree than would have seemed probable to many critics; it came from a certain fear" (p. 69).

In 1881 Isabel Archer exercises an acute sensibility which, in the following decades, matures into the perversity of the decadent movement. Although she never displays the nervous energy of a Des Esseintes, she seems attracted to his world. Perhaps as much as anything else that is what the fateful descent into marriage with Osmond suggests. However attractive and promising she may be, Isabel Archer is not the blossom of red-blooded American girlhood she may seem. An isolating imagination and a nascent symbolist tendency of seeing luminosity in the void are tempered with darkness, morbidity, hermetic seclusion, frigidity, and even the inhuman connoisseurship of an Osmond or a Des Esseintes. She seeks in marriage "the finest individual," but the New York Edition intensifies the frigid aestheticism of her selectivity by having Isabel choose "the finest manly organism she had ever known."[9] Isabel Archer remains a worthy heroine, but her flaws are complex. Her husband may display a wraithlike wrist, but she shares many gestures with him. Her life unfolds in a misty *fin-de-siècle* atmosphere which was to stifle many people who found themselves ambivalently poised between positive and negative, between darkness and light, and sometimes between polarities of sexuality.

When Isabel leaves England, in part fleeing from Warburton and Goodwood, she travels to a Rome which is nothing like the image of rich redundancy it was for Roderick Hudson. Isabel finds in the Eternal City a place where she might withdraw from life, as she withdrew in

Albany. Despite all the superficial splendor, she once again has retired to a symbolist chamber.

> She sat down in the middle of the circle of statues, looking at them vaguely, resting her eyes on their beautiful blank faces; listening, as it were, to their eternal silence. It is impossible in Rome at least, to look long at a great company of Greek sculptures without feeling the effect of their noble quietude. It soothes and moderates the spirit, it purifies the imagination. I say in Rome especially, because the Roman air is an exquisite medium for such impressions. The golden sunshine mingles with them, the great stillness of the past, so vivid yet, though it is nothing but a void full of names, seems to throw a solemn spell upon them. [p. 263]

Isabel Archer faces the silent structural portal once again. The young woman from New York thinks she is heading in the direction of vitality and freedom, but each step she takes draws her closer to the ambiguous quietude of Gilbert Osmond.

There are no easy answers here. If the reader understands the position of the novel's heroine as fundamentally opposed to that of Roderick Hudson, Isabel wedding herself to a husband who exists as entity solely through imaginative exercise, Hudson attaching himself to a woman whose phenomenological richness annihilates any imaginative exercise, failure comes both ways. Nonetheless, Isabel develops as the stronger of the two. Hudson marries the real thing; Isabel fears it and marries a man who might protect her from confronting it and being consumed by it. She becomes an institutional John Marcher, still waiting, fearfully if reluctantly, for the white lightning that comes at the end.

In *The American* the silence of the Bellegardes exerts barely negative pressure, but in *Portrait* Osmond seems clearly vicious, and James indicates far less admiration for the increasingly withdrawn and increasingly quiet life. In 1881 James completed another work on a similar theme of malignancy. Silence in *The American* may have been a general mixture of the gracious and the stubborn, but in *Washington Square* Dr. Sloper's silence develops as a fully manipulative force. His daughter may not be an attractive young woman, but otherwise she is much like the weak-willed Pansy Osmond, and she too is terrified of her father. Quiet, inscrutable, a discriminating gentleman who is superficially the ideal of civilized concern, Dr. Sloper exercises a control which is nearly as inhuman as Osmond's.

Silence as pressure—powerfully developed in our own time in the plays of Harold Pinter—finds expression in the second paragraph of *Washington Square* when the doctor's influence over his patients is indicated by the fact that he "sometimes explained matters . . . [but] he never went so far (like some practitioners one has heard of) as to trust the explanation alone, but always left behind him an inscrutable prescription."[10] The near-silence of inscrutable statement is the foundation of Sloper's dominance, over patients, over people in general, and particularly over his daughter. He remains strong and nearly invulnerable as long as he says little or nothing and as long as he never makes his desires explicit. He leaves much unstated, and such a practice works heavily even on the tender, if rather weak, imagination of his sluggardly daughter.

For almost half the book he refrains from openly forbidding Catherine to see Townsend. His treatment is remote and it leaves his daughter haunted, pitiable, powerless. After returning from her meeting with Morris in Washington Square park, she soon feels her father's pressure.

> . . . going home with her father, and feeling him near, the poor girl, in spite of her sudden declaration of courage, began to tremble again. Her father said nothing; but she had an idea his eyes were fixed upon her in the darkness. [*WS*, p. 84]

With discipline sufficient to keep significant words to himself, he talks only about irrelevant matters and then he speaks with cool fluidity. His decision is wise and he comprehends his wisdom. Catherine, desperate to confront her father's disapproval, asks, "You mean that he is a mercenary?"

> Her father looked up at her still, with his cold, quiet, reasonable eye. "If I meant it, my dear, I should say it! But there is an error I wish particularly to avoid—that of rendering Mr. Townsend more interesting to you by saying hard things about him." [*WS*, p. 98]

The clever doctor does not make his disapproval explicit. He knows, however, that Aunt Penniman and her niece feel the weight of his unspoken recriminations—"They are both afraid of me, harmless as I am," the Doctor says. "And it is on that I build—on the salutary terror I inspire" (WS, p. 98).

For the most part, whenever the doctor must say something of any significance, when he confronts a crucial question and cannot, decently or politely, keep silent, his most potent words provide little more than structural silences which give up neutral and obstinately opaque reactions. When Catherine asks if she may see Morris Townsend again, Dr. Sloper answers, "Just as you choose." She says she *will* see the young man again, and her father answers, "Exactly as you choose." She counters that it will be only for the present and he repeats, "Exactly as you choose" (WS, pp. 136–39). Although he offers speech, the oddity of his syntax, without verbal reference to his own feelings, returns her statement with the muteness of tautology. Catherine breaks into tears and flees the room.

As long as his declarations are kept suggestive, but indistinct, they are effective, for even the mild imagination of Catherine Sloper invests them with sufficient horror. But Dr. Sloper loses control—as Osmond almost never will and as Maggie Verver never will. His frustration with an insistent attachment grows and he becomes explicit. As he does, Catherine becomes less frightened. As he begins to forbid, she begins to defy. She meets the worst realities in the words her father utters and she finds the *stated* worst inexpressibly easier to bear than the unstated opprobrium. The real thing, in words or in flesh, claims less energy than the quiet or the approximately quiet.

Dr. Sloper grows definite, and as he does his daughter gains courage. At first he tells Morris he will not be the forbidding "father in an old-fashioned novel" (WS, p. 93), but in time he becomes that and more. He abandons silences for words and eventually for physical intimidation. He takes his daughter to Europe and atop a Swiss mountain "abruptly in a low tone, he asked her an abrupt question, 'Have you given him up?' " She says she has not and her father shows more fury than he ever has before.

> "I am very angry."
>
> She wondered what he meant—whether he wished to frighten her. If he did, the place was well chosen; this hard, melancholy dell, abandoned by the summer light, made her feel her loneliness. She looked around her, and her heart grew cold; for a moment her fear was great. . . . The place was ugly and lonely, but the place could do her no harm. There was a

kind of still intensity about her father which made him dangerous, but Catherine hardly went so far as to say to herself that it might be part of his plan to fasten his hand—the neat, fine, supple hand of a distinguished physician—in her throat. Nevertheless, she receded a step. . . .

The Doctor looked round him too. "Should you like to be left in such a place as this, to starve?" [WS, pp. 177–79]

The abstract coldness, hardness, cruelty, and remoteness of Sloper's silent moments here compress into concrete explicit threat. Catherine trembles momentarily. Then she speaks out against him and realizes that "she made her way forward with difficulty, her heart beating with the excitement of having for the first time spoken to him in violence" (WS, p. 179). From this moment, after her father's grand lapse into words, Catherine Sloper becomes her own woman. The irony asserts itself; when openly, explicitly, verbally and almost physically Dr. Sloper becomes the real thing of old-fashioned novels, no longer quiet and malevolently benign, he loses power. Finally, enfeebled and waiting to die, he commits his most definite words to the legal document of his will, and there the forbidding words stand, clear, codified, irrefutable forever, entirely free from any imaginative exercise; Catherine cares nothing for them. Far from being shaken by the harshness of the will, she tells Aunt Penniman, "I like it very much" (WS, p. 250).

The effect of Sloper's grim silence on his sluggardly daughter nearly devastates her. The reader might appreciate the effect of a similar force on the imaginatively gifted Isabel Archer. "Suffering," for Isabel, "was an active condition; it was not a chill, a stupor, a despair; it was passion of thought, of speculation" (p. 372). Increasingly, James demonstrates how the imaginative mind—Isabel's, but certainly Madame Merle's—responds richly to absences, first to invest Osmond with positive value, then to invest his silences with malevolence. Osmond, like Dr. Sloper, builds his salutary terror, but he keeps surer control and maintains his house as stiller than that on Washington Square.

She could live it over again, the incredulous terror with which she had taken the measure of her dwelling. Between those four walls she had lived ever since; they were to surround her for the rest of her life. It was the house of darkness, the house of dumbness, the house of suffocation. [p. 375]

Isabel Archer faces indefinite, unspoken opposition and, as Osmond's scornful silent pressure works upon her imagination, she finds almost no way out of a dense conjugal claustrophobia. In *The Golden Bowl* Maggie Verver offers such a system; Charlotte will nearly disintegrate under the pressure of Maggie's sustained silence and she will escape, like Madame Merle, only by fleeing to America. In *Portrait*, however, the power is darker and less surely understood.

> She knew of no wrong that he had done; he was not violent, he was not cruel; she simply believed that he hated her. That was all she accused him of, and the miserable part of it was precisely that it was not a crime, for against a crime she might have found redress. . . . He would, if possible, never give her a pretext, never put himself in the wrong. Isabel, scanning the future with dry, fixed eyes, saw that he would have the better of her there. [p. 372]

When their break finally comes at the end, Henrietta Stackpole asks, "Did your husband make a scene about your coming?"

> "No; I can't say he made a scene."
> "He didn't object then?"
> "Yes, he objected very much. But it was not what you'd call a scene."
> "What was it then?"
> "It was a very quiet conversation."
> Henrietta for a moment contemplated her guest. "It must have been hellish," she then remarked. [pp. 495–96]

With his constant "objections" (p. 405), his "sore, mute protest" in the New York Edition,[11] Gilbert Osmond powerfully opposes his wife; she finds her hope crushed.

> Instead of leading to the high places of happiness, from which the world would seem to lie below one, so that one could look down with a sense of exaltation and advantage, and judge and choose and pity, it led rather downward and earthward, into realms of restriction and depression, where the sound of other

lives, easier and freer, was heard from above, and served to deepen the feeling of failure. [pp. 371–72]

A moderately perverse happiness defines itself in terms of such ego-tistical superiority—exalting, judging, pitying, condescending to the species below. Ultimately Isabel shares the egotism of Osmond. Failure seems inevitable, and that consequent failure characteristically evolves in opposition to metaphors of positivistic sound as freedom.

Osmond's tense control remains almost unbroken in the novel; when he finally does speak—and he speaks only a few words—indefinite terms provide the implication of the unstated more than the declared. Isabel recoils with dramatic sexual disgust when Osmond tells her that he believes she can influence Lord Warburton to marry Pansy—" 'Well,' he said, 'I hold that it lies in your hands. I shall leave it there. With a little good-will you may manage it. Think that over and remember that I count upon you' " (p. 369). The entirety of the next long chapter, Chapter XLII, records Isabel intellectually reeling, and it traces her mute considerations of these vague words, so polite and casual, and, if threat at all, the most elusive of threats. His is the quietest injunction; her reaction is tremendous—there "were certain things she could never take in. To begin with they were hideously unclean. She was not a daughter of the Puritans, but for all that she believed in such a thing as purity. It would appear that Osmond didn't; some of his traditions made her push back her skirts" (p. 378).

Nothing Osmond has said has come close to the force of anything "hideously unclean" or of, ambiguously, causing the pushing back of one's skirts, but Isabel invests monstrosity in Osmond's quiet parting remark. Susan Sontag has described how, "when punctuated by long silences, words weigh more; they become almost palpable,"[12] and indeed Osmond's unspeaking habit makes every spoken word, no matter how casual, a revelation. Isabel then wonders, "Did all women have lovers?", and the New York Edition intensifies the sexual reference with a shift of concern from "purity" to concern for "chastity and decency."[13] If Gilbert Osmond's intention is to suggest to his wife that she offer herself to Warburton in exchange for a promise of marriage with Pansy, Osmond barely breathes the suggestion. Its force would seem palpable nonethe-less. He counts on his wife's imagination—the imagination of "the most imaginative women he had known"—to bridge the half-silence he has provided. Of course she can say nothing. In no way can Isabel voice her interpretation to her husband. He would only deny, in horror, and she would lose everything.

Somewhat like Christopher Newman, Isabel Archer learns that even the clever words of Madame Merle and Osmond are dead ciphers compared to the intensity of their silences; a great scene helps bring about this understanding. She suddenly returns to her house in Rome.

> Just beyond the threshold of the drawing-room she stopped short, the reason for her doing so being that she had received an impression. The impression had, in strictness, nothing unprecedented; but she felt it as something new, and the soundlessness of her step gave her time to take in the scene before she interrupted it. Madame Merle sat there in her bonnet, and Gilbert Osmond was talking to her; for a minute they were unaware that she had come in. Isabel had often seen that before, certainly; but what she had not seen, or at least had not noticed—was that their dialogue had for the moment converted itself into a sort of familiar silence, from which she instantly perceived that her entrance would startle them. Madame Merle was standing on the rug, a little way from the fire; Osmond was in a deep chair, leaning back and looking at her. Her head was erect, as usual, but her eyes were bent upon his. What struck Isabel first was that he was sitting while Madame Merle stood; there was an anomaly in this that arrested her. Then she perceived that they had arrived at a desultory pause in their exchange of ideas, and were musing, face to face, with the freedom of old friends who sometimes exchange ideas without uttering them. [p. 357]

Isabel's growing perception of wordless communication begins to crack the facade of talk and concern which has been Madame Merle's construction. Later, when long into the night her mind wanders, she considers what she saw—"But even then she stopped again in the middle of the room, and stood there gazing at a remembered vision—that of her husband and Madame Merle, grouped unconsciously and familiarly associated." Restrained and pregnant, such moments are more common to the gesture of French theater than to American fiction. Diderot spoke of such intensity when he wrote to Voltaire, "J'ai dans la tête un moment de théâtre où tout est muet, et où le spectateur reste suspendu dans les plus terribles alarmes" [I have in my mind a theatrical moment when all is mute, and when the spectator stands gripped in the most terrible alarm].[14]

At times James's fiction prefigures the Continental "théâtre d'attente" and the "théâtre du silence."[15] Isabel Archer in the doorway grows aware of what Maeterlinck claimed as a key truth in his personal symbolist manifesto *The Treasure of the Humble*, that "words may pass between men, but let silence have its instant of activity and it will never efface itself, and indeed the true life, the only life that leaves a trace behind, is made up of silence alone."[16] In the stance at the portal, in the theatricality of its tableau, and particularly in the comprehension of the wordless exchange in desultory pause, there is the sense of what Maeterlinck repeatedly dramatized, that "it is idle to think that, by means of words, any real communication can pass from one man to another."[17]

The same cultural atmosphere which nourished Maeterlinck stirred James's imagination, although the dramatist's work did not begin to appear until the late 1880s. In 1902 the narrator of *The Wings of the Dove* reports that Susan Stringham definitely had read her Maeterlinck and Pater, and there are several other direct references to Maeterlinck in the late fiction. A happy coincidence comes when, in an interview in the middle of his career, Maeterlinck declares that the poet might best of all consider "l'ordre mystérieux et éternel et la force occulte des choses,"[18] stirring the same vibrations as Isabel Archer wondering at "the eternal mystery of things." Maeterlinck's earliest English translator, Richard Hovey, once wrote that the dramatist's "master-tone is always terror,"[19] and certainly the increasingly tense silences of both writers inform with intense fear.

Along with the terrors comes a loss of faith in language. In 1920 Wittgenstein would assert, in Steiner's words, the view that "that which we call fact may well be a veil spun by language to shroud the mind from reality."[20] In 1881 Isabel Archer increasingly suspects the irrelevance of words—"And it seemed to her an act of devotion to conceal her misery from [Ralph]. She concealed it elaborately; in their talk she was perpetually hanging out curtains and arranging screens" (p. 380). Only for brief moments does she exert newly discerned power.

She and Madame Merle meet for the last time, and another silence, more electric if less meaningful than the one at the portal, widens the crack in the polished surface and dictates Madame Merle's retreat.

So Madame Merle went on, with much of the brilliancy of
a woman who had long been a mistress of the art of conversation. But there were phases and gradations in her speech,
not one of which was lost upon Isabel's ear, though her eyes
were absent from her companion's face. She had not proceeded
far before Isabel noted a sudden rupture in her voice, which
was in itself a complete drama. This subtle modulation marked
a momentous discovery—the perception of an entirely new
attitude on the part of her listener. Madame Merle had guessed
in the space of an instant that everything was at an end between
them, and in the space of another instant she had guessed the
reason why. The person who stood there was not the same
one she had seen hitherto; it was a very different person—a
person who knew her secret. This discovery was tremendous,
and for the moment she made it the most accomplished of
women faltered and lost her courage. But only for that moment.
Then the conscious stream of her perfect manner gathered
itself again and flowed on as smoothly as might be to the end.
But it was only because she had the end in view that she was
able to go on. She had been touched with a point that made
her quiver, and she needed all the alertness of her will to
repress her agitation. Her only safety was in her not betraying
herself. She did not betray herself; but the startled quality of
her voice refused to improve—she couldn't help it—while she
heard herself say she hardly knew what. The tide of her confidence ebbed, and she was able only just to glide into port,
faintly grazing the bottom. [pp. 483–84]

The break in the voice, the lapse in continuity, provides the complete
drama. The *words* of Madame Merle are not reported here, for the
report of such phenomena would appear irrelevant. Isabel reads significance in the gaps, breaks, silences, and she holds her own speech
back to gain power—although she almost breaks into words and loses
the scene. Isabel offers Madame Merle a response not unlike the malevolent blankness her husband has offered throughout their marriage.

There was a moment during which, if she had turned and
spoken, she would have said something that would hiss like a
lash. But she closed her eyes, and then the hideous vision died
away. What remained was the cleverest woman in the world,

standing there within a few feet of her and knowing as little
what to think as the meanest. Isabel's only revenge was to be
silent still. [p. 484]

In quiet battle Isabel forcefully acts, exerting pressure by remaining
motionless.

> She left her there for a period which must have seemed long
> to this lady, who at last seated herself with a movement which
> was in itself a confession of helplessness. Then Isabel turned
> her eyes and looked down at her. Madame Merle was very
> pale; her own eyes covered Isabel's face. She might see what
> she would, but her danger was over. Isabel would never accuse
> her, never reproach her; perhaps because she would never give
> her the opportunity to defend herself. [p. 484]

It was said that "Madame Merle was rarely guilty of the awkwardness
of retracting what she had said; her wisdom was shown rather in maintaining it and placing it in a favourable light" (p. 182). Isabel Archer's
refusal to comment deprives Madame Merle—the brilliant "mistress of
the art of conversation"—of the opportunity to exercise her particular
wisdom. Isabel never accuses Madame Merle and never reveals how
much she knows of Osmond's relationship with her. The unyielding
silence on the supreme sensitivity of Madame Merle creates immeasurable tension for the older woman—"Madame Merle raised her eyes.
'I shall go to America,' she announced" (p. 491).

The pattern of wordless moments in *Portrait* moves toward the most
troublesome silence in the novel. In a notebook entry James himself
commented upon the notable problem of the abrupt ending—"The
obvious criticism of course will be that it is not finished—that I have
not seen the heroine to the end of her situation—that I have left her
en l'air—This is both true and false. The whole of anything is never
told; you can only take what groups together."[21] *The Portrait of a Lady*
"groups" the way it does for several reasons. Finally Isabel Archer returns
to her mute marriage in Rome. When Isabel quietly sits alone long
into the night, "motionlessly seeing," her consciousness matures. In
Philip Weinstein's view, "Isabel's 'extraordinary meditative vigil' is
presented as one of her most intense adventures; the more 'expected'
scenes of emotion and intimacy—her union with Osmond, her increasingly horrified glimpses into his real character, the birth and death of

her baby—are passed over without mention in the four-year break between chapters xxv and xxvi."[22] Her active experience, here nascent and barely articulated, will be relived by Milly Theale, who in a moment of epiphanic fulfillment will experience the "adventure of not stirring."[23] For the most part, however, the silences at the end of *Portrait* suggest frigidity.

Nonetheless, James's not taking the reader to Rome, his not allowing the reader to observe the encounter between Osmond and his wife, provides a successful conclusion. In Albany, Isabel faced a "silent, motionless portal," and what lay on the other side "became to the child's imagination, according to its different moods, a region of delight or of terror." That doorway provided the focus for an immature imagination, but the one through which Isabel passes at the end—through which the reader never passes—leads to an inexorably more silent place where the mature consciousness will exercise full subtlety. The tense silence she encounters in Rome reverberates with complex pulses alien to the poetic fantasies of Albany. Joseph Conrad appreciated the fine silences of Henry James more than did most writers. He wrote that:

> Perhaps the only true desire of mankind, coming thus to light in its hour of leisure, is to be set at rest. One is never set at rest by Mr. Henry James's novels. His books end as an episode in life ends. You remain with the sense of life still going on; and even the subtle presence of the dead is felt in the silence that comes upon the artist-creation when the last word has been read.[24]

The book groups with symmetry. It begins in a doorway which leads to chatter on lawns, laughter over tea, an opening, according to William Gass, "on rich sounds,"[25] a lovely, languid, attentuated, pathetic, enervated world. It ends with the flight through the final portal to grim silence beyond, which, ironically, charges with intensity.

The nineteenth century's retreat from positivism nourished a rarefied race whose brave new world would flourish when experience was met, not by scientific method but by rich imagination, delicate discriminations, and occult hypersensitivity. Isabel Archer's revolt against the redundant actuality of a Lord Warburton has the force of the symbolist's rejection of concreteness, and not so strangely it carries her into the chamber of the decadents. Pissarro among others had feared that the "truth" of impressionism might be replaced by the very kind of escapist aestheticism with which Isabel views her ghostly husband.[26] Robert Goldwater has called the silent presences the epitome of symbolist intent and indeed they consistently provide the focus of Isabel Archer's perceptions. *The Portrait of a Lady* explores the dangers of the modernist imagination as it turns to the quiet portals of a new age and finds too late that they often may be barren walls. One of the first to project upon the void a falsely rich life, Isabel Archer develops as the first major heroine in Henry James who deeply feels the pressure of the unspoken. She fails, however, to exert very much force, and she remains an immature consciousness throughout the novel. Therefore she is a victim—of others and of herself.

The American heiress may be haunted by the ghosts of the symbolists, but the entirely different heroine of *The Spoils of Poynton* begins as a cleverly disguised daughter of the century's materialism, a product of the negligible and sooty London suburbs. Her icons are splendid marble statues, not ghostly non-presences, and her quest seems bluntly for an embarrassment of riches as art, up to the rafters and out into the hall. Her disinherited condition may give her the cast of the wandering poetess, but she actually has nothing to do with the garret, for as hungrily as any American collector she wants the real physical thing in her grasp. Yeats would write of the symbolist struggle to know the dance from the dancer, but the discriminatory task is as difficult with gold, ivory, and alabaster as with the tapering of a limb. *The Spoils of Poynton* in part explores the over-materialization of art: where the dance is the dancer, where suggestive silences are swallowed up by the great chorus, and where there is the ranging of Philistines—obvious or less obvious—followed by the gathering of spoils which have been left behind in heaps.

Here James evolves new relationships, pitting flesh against spirit and words against silence, and for a time the struggle holds in deadlock. When the smoke clears and the spoils are counted out, honor and asceticism seem the losers. Barbarians sweep through the house, take captives, and then roar off to the continent. Fleda Vetch seems to fail, and some readers will call her, with Kenneth Graham, "a disguised New England heroine . . . the equivalent of that American social penury James associated elsewhere with self-consuming spiritualities."[27] But her consciousness matures and she almost succeeds. "Let yourself go!" wails Mrs. Gereth, but the large physical presence of Mona Brigstock lets itself go first. Fleda may seem to fail because she too quietly restrains herself, too long, but she matures as the first of a late sisterhood that will hold back and exert sure, complex power. Their silences become action, and no house burns before Milly Theale or Maggie Verver. Both heroines are called "priestesses" as they soundlessly move through their *palazzi*, but Fleda's quiet method is only half-formed, and "her silence was an acceptance as responsible as the vow of a nun."[28]

Eventually the unpossessing and unprepossessing young woman travels back to Poynton. The scene would be ripe for her movement through the empty rooms—like Milly Theale, "to and fro as the priestess of worship"—the surveying of beauty, the approach to the Maltese Cross and its elevation in a ceremonial gesture. In so doing Fleda might fulfill a novitiate and her trial of silence might end. But the house burns, as does all it represents, and the poor girl must take the most negative path and pull away from even the most subtle materiality. Susan Sontag has spoken of such progress: "As the activity of the mystic must end in a *via negativa*, a theology of God's absence, a craving for the cloud of unknowing beyond knowledge and for silence beyond speech, so art must tend toward anti-art, the elimination of the 'subject' (the 'object,' the 'image'), the substitution of chance for intention, and the pursuit of silence."[29] Fleda Vetch perhaps begins her most important journey when, at the end, instead of finding her splendid prize, she draws the stench of smoke into her nostrils.

It is easy to condemn this young woman with a bloodless name as fussy and frigid, as a too-punctilious spirit who stupidly fails to fight the attraction of flesh and blood that Mona Bristock represents. The lesson seems clear—she should have held back neither words nor emotions. Yet two later heroines hold back and no one condemns Milly Theale and few condemn Maggie Verver. The dignity of the dying heiress derives from her reserve until death, and if the married heiress had said what she knew, the foully interlocking world around the Ververs would have exploded.

The Spoils of Poynton describes the re-education of a well-formed creature who has an exquisite taste for worldliness—"a hungry girl whose sensibility was almost as great as her opportunities had been small" (p. 26). Early on, Mrs. Gereth and Miss Vetch meet as kindred spirits who feel the same about everything, about the horrors of antimacassars, Waterbath, and Mona. Mrs. Gereth is "struck with the acuteness of the little girl who had put a finger on her hidden string" (p. 5). They think alike and both agree that " 'Things' were of course the sum of the world" (p. 27). Such rawly practical vision is at the heart of the wave of scientism which had swept the nineteenth century—and which

James had opposed from the beginning of his career—although here it transfers to the subtly seductive incarnations of aestheticised materialism. Fleda and Mrs. Gereth begin with such an organizing principle, but by the end of the book they are separated and the young woman has developed a different sensibility. No longer do the pair occultly trip the same springs and eye each other meaningfully from across rooms filled with extravagant ugliness. Fleda Vetch eventually begins to move away from the more apparent phenomenology of Poynton.

Poynton at first appears the goal of a life, and for a time Fleda works to obtain the exquisite plenitude it represents, just as Merton Densher plots for plenty with Kate Croy. In *The Wings of the Dove* Densher discovers that Milly Theale's absence becomes the great force of his life, greater than the wealth of ages shared with an English beauty. Both Fleda Vetch and Densher end up empty-handed, but not empty. Finally Kate Croy claims, justly, that Densher is in love with Milly's ghost. Initially when Fleda viewed Poynton she bluntly "gave herself up to satiety. Preoccupations and scruples fell away from her" (p. 24). At the end of *The Spoils of Poynton* Fleda too retains a ghost, and she recognizes that suggestive absences can matter as positive values. Things, or phenomena, are nothing like the sum of the world.

Finally Fleda visits Ricks, the little country house which Mrs. Gereth inherited from a maiden aunt. Fleda remarks at how wonderful that ordinary house has turned out under the inspired hand of Mrs. Gereth.

> " . . . You've only to be a day or two at a place with four sticks for something to come of it!"
>
> "Then if anything has come of it here, it has come precisely of just four. That's literally, by the inventory, all there are!" said Mrs. Gereth.
>
> "If there were more there would be too many to convey the impression in which half the beauty resides—the impression, somehow, of something dreamed and missed, something reduced, relinquished, resigned: the poetry, as it were, of something sensibly *gone*." Fleda ingeniously and triumphantly worked it out. "Ah, there's something here that will never be in the inventory!"
>
> "Does it happen to be in your power to give it a name?" Mrs. Gereth's face showed the dim dawn of an amusement at finding herself seated at the feet of her pupil.

"I can give it a dozen. It's a kind of fourth dimension. It's a presence, a perfume, a touch. It's a soul, a story, a life. There's ever so much more here than you and I. We're in fact just three!" [pp. 302–03]

Fleda speaks here of a "fourth dimension," a fecundated absence at the heart of many values in the novels. Mrs. Gereth answers, "Oh, if you count ghosts!"

"Of course I count ghosts. It seems to me ghosts count double—for what they were and for what they are. Somehow there were no ghosts at Poynton," Fleda went on. "That was the only fault." [p. 303]

A nascent symbolist consciousness discovers the rare "poetry, as it were, of something sensibly *gone*" and that discovery begins to offer excitement which rivals the rather shallow charms of Mrs. Gereth's son.

Christopher Newman held out in silence and waited for the Bellegardes to break under the threat of scandal. He kept quiet. They kept quiet. Claire finally withdrew and he tossed the incriminating letter into the fire. He never let himself go, although he might have gotten his bride if he had. Fleda Vetch resembles the grander heroines of the major phase, but her discipline links her to heroes as early as Newman. Both keep tense silences, both misjudge the effect of those silences, both lose their lovers. Both are told that their more worldly-wise rivals counted on their reticence all along. Even the last touches are similar. Newman tosses the damning note into the fire and turns to find nothing left of it. Fleda returns to find Poynton consumed by flames.

The serious games Christopher Newman and Fleda Vetch play are not substantially different, although the young woman's actions are not, like Newman's, prompted by "remarkable good nature." If readers generally approve of the gentlemen's nobility because he does not "let himself go" and announce the Bellegardes' crime, while they pity Fleda, it may be because Newman goes home to raw wealth. But the fortune should not create an artificial distinction; Fleda's non-action takes considerably more courage, and the honorable silences she keeps—and she keeps several with far more serious intention than simple good nature— point in a new direction.

Fleda Vetch gives up a life with Owen Gereth which she could have claimed had she told Mrs. Gereth that *never* would Mona marry her son without the pictures, the art, all the artifacts—Mona would say, "in that voice like the squeeze of a doll's stomach: 'it goes with the house—it goes with the house' " (p. 19). Fleda holds back and she grows morally. She begins as something of a professional guest among the monied folk, even if she despises them and maliciously laughs behind their backs. The two high ladies—"the wiseheads" (p. 23) the narrator calls them—are rather despicable guests in someone else's home.

> There was in the elder lady's [room] a set of comic water-colors, a family joke by a family genius, and in the younger's a souvenir from some centennial or other Exhibition, that they shudderingly alluded to. The house was perversely full of souvenirs of places even more ugly than itself and of things it would have been a pious duty to forget. The worst horror was the acres of varnish, something advertised and smelly, with which everything was smeared; it was Fleda Vetch's conviction that the application of it, by their own hand and hilariously shoving each other, was the amusement of the Brigstocks on rainy days. [p. 6]

Flannery O'Connor is right when she says that the vulgar family is so much nicer than the artistic pair who archly scan the spectacle before them;[30] she believes that James was making fun of the heroine throughout, and perhaps it is so. The young woman who emerges at the end of the novel transcends the mean young connoisseur at the beginning, for she begins to perceive the ironic emptiness of Poynton and she finds other values.

If the book is a comedy, as some critics claim, it is hardly of the drawing room where fancy people offer barbs with tea. The great comedy is the lugging of furniture—out of Poynton, into Ricks, with clocks and pictures up to the ceiling, and then summoning the movers back and lugging more. The reader appreciates relatively little no art. There is reference to the Maltese cross, but only reference, and often art is powerfully presented in Henry James, from the exciting pieces Roderick Hudson fashions, to "Murillo's beautifully moon-borne Madonna" on the first page of The American, to the central importance of the extraordinary Bronzino portrait of Lucrezia Panciatichi in The Wings of the Dove. The Spoils of Poynton provides the battle for a magnificent house, but it evokes no beautiful things and the reader senses no objective correlative but the contents of lorries and vans, bickered over, packed, hoisted and carted over the green English hills. The book may talk about beautiful things but the beauty is not there nearly as much as is the detritus of positivism and greedy materialism.

The possible pun of the title suggests that something is rotten in the rich wood and ormolu of Poynton and it takes Fleda considerable time before she sniffs its pungency. She eventually shifts her attention from "things," the preoccupation of her first train ride when she was greedy for "neither more nor less than the things with which she had had time to learn from Mrs. Gereth that Poynton overflowed." At the end of the novel, after her ordeal of silence she reaches a stage where "things" fall away. Almost completely dispossessed of the house, just before it burns she makes an imaginative leap for the first time, and in its absence she fully possesses the place.

> She moved there in thought—in the great rooms she knew; she should be able to say to herself that, for once at least, her possession was as complete as that of either of the others whom it had filled only with bitterness. And a thousand times yes— her choice should know no scruple: the thing she should go down to take would be up to the height of her privilege. The whole place was in her eyes. [p. 316]

For all the talk of the material beauty of Poynton, the house does not work for life. One should not take too lightly the vicious split between mother and son due to "things"—and that is the word, which, flat and vulgar as it sounds, constantly names the contents of the house. Mother steals from son and son visits solicitors; in an uneasy way the fiancée offers herself up for the price of sofas. Even when Mrs. Gereth brags of her refinement, the reader might grow uneasy. She speaks of her "patience, an almost infernal cunning."

> They had saved on lots of things in life, and there were lots of things they hadn't had, but they had had in every corner of Europe their swing among the Jews. It was fascinating to poor Fleda, who hadn't a penny in the world nor anything nice at home, and whose only treasure was her subtle mind, to hear this genuine English lady, fresh and fair, young in the fifties, declare with gayety and conviction that she was herself the greatest Jew who ever tracked her victim. [p. 14]

There is too much Shylock in Mrs. Gereth. Art becomes accumulation, materialism, uneasy obsession; it blurs with money and corruption sets in. Poynton begins in the bargaining rooms of questionable markets, and there should be little expectation that it might end with the uplifting of a sacred cross, which, surely, must burn with the house.

Poynton resembles the hermitage of Tennyson's "Palace of Art," a poem which Henry James had discussed in his essay on "Mr. Tennyson's Drama."[31] Anyone who spends too much time walled up by the objects of art becomes ripe for debilitating egotism, disassociation from reality, and a habit of unappealing contempt for more vigorous human impulses—those not far from the heart of Waterbath and the Brigstocks.

> "O God-like isolation which art mine,
>   I can but count thee perfect gain,
> What time I watch the darkening droves of swine
>   That range on yonder plain."
>
> "In filthy sloughs they roll a prurient skin,
>   They graze and wallow, breed and sleep;
> And oft some brainless devil enters in,
>   And drives them to the deep."

In Tennyson's poem the temple of art is struck down, and in both works a conflagration suggests refinement as much as loss. "The Palace of Art" ends with the following:

> "Make me a cottage in the vale," she said,
>   "Where I may mourn and pray.
>
> "Yet pull not down my palace towers, that are
>   So lightly, beautifully built:
> Perchance I may return with others there
>   When I have purged my guilt."[32]

Eventually Fleda prefers the atmosphere of Ricks, quiet, suggestive, and vacant. Poynton is too loud, too rich, but the retired cottage allows expression which Mrs. Gereth, bemoaning the loss of "the great chorus of Poynton," cannot hear. "You're not," Fleda tells her friend, "I'm sure, either so proud or so broken to be reached by nothing but that. This is a voice so gentle, so human, so feminine—a faint far-away voice with a little quiver of heart-break" (pp. 301–2). Like the woman at the end of Tennyson's poem, Fleda Vetch must be purged of a subtly destructive plenitude, and the movement of the novel is toward final purification by fire.

Yet Mrs. Gereth admits that when she had removed herself for twenty-five years to Poynton, "life had become for her a kind of fool's paradise. She couldn't leave her house without peril of exposure" (p. 13). Although when Fleda first visited Poynton, she gave herself up to "satiety," eventually the house worked against her as much as Rome worked against Roderick Hudson.

> Poynton moreover had been an impossible place for producing; no active art could flourish there but a Buddhistic contemplation. It had stripped its mistress clean of all feeble accomplishments; her hands were imbrued neither with ink nor watercolor. [p. 176]

And the revised New York Edition intensifies the questionable influence of Poynton with "her hand had sooner been imbrued with blood than with ink or water-color." For all its surface richness, Poynton generates little more than sterility, or bloody destruction, and Fleda's failure—and it is a true failure—is that she learns a lesson too late.

Finally Mrs. Gereth writes to her friend, "You don't understand quite everything, but of all my acquaintance you're far away the least stupid. For action you're no good at all; but action is over, for me" (p. 297). Not entirely wrong in her evaluation, Mrs. Gereth is mostly wrong. If action means "to let yourself go," then Fleda Vetch has failed. But James explores modes of action which only superficially seem like stillnesses. Significant activity in the fiction rarely shows as broad gestures or shifting of loins. *The Spoils of Poynton* extends the view, in "The Art of Fiction," of experience as perception; it explores passivity as action itself. Fleda Vetch's abstention from pressure on Owen, and her refusal to speak out to Mrs. Gereth are the major forces of the novel. Action defines as non-action, and the tense silence Fleda keeps—although it does not yet bring success to a heroine—becomes the purest pressure she might exert without making offense against human freedom. Her silence works within the pattern of ironies in the novel—a palace of art, teeming with beautiful things and ringing out with a great chorus, turns out something dead on the heath, while quiet and retired

Ricks fills with the poetry of life. In abstention Fleda Vetch begins to find vitality.

The Spoils of Poynton develops silence as faltering but benevolent moral force. Not empty renunciation, it exists in the space between dumb passivity and manipulation, a passivity which comes close to the ignorant good nature of Christopher Newman, a manipulative force not unlike that of Dr. Sloper or Maggie Verver. Fleda Vetch's silence is still a faltering action, but it is the fundamental method of a heroine who is more vigorous at the end. Like the speaker of Tennyson's "Palace of Art," Fleda Vetch seems "on fire within," even if for the present the overwhelming physical force of Mona Brigstock claims the spoils.

Isabel Archer and Fleda Vetch attempt extreme and opposite marriages. An American heiress preoccupied with both the anti-phenomenology of the symbolists and the negativism of the decadents unites with a blank cipher upon whom she fully might exercise her imagination. A subtle English girl—eager child of the century's heroic materialism—initially works to wed a man who represents things as the positivistic sum of the world, but her phenomenological passion lays too many sacrifices on the altar of a suspiciously mercantile taste. Isabel Archer and Fleda Vetch demonstrate the risks of refined sensibilities which develop contrary obsessions, for the silent portal or for the great chorus behind the door. Fleda Vetch never attains the stature of the spirited woman from Albany, but her final path may seem surer than the dark return to Rome.

Her recognition of vitality in "something sensibly gone" brings her close to Isabel Archer's early assertion that a house where many have died is a house full of life. In 1897, however, James has not come full circle, for Fleda Vetch's imagination exercises control that Isabel's did not. Isabel Archer eventually invests life in the utterly lifeless, in the ghoulish far more than in the ghostly, and her motives would seem fundamentally, and subtly, egotistical. Fleda Vetch's creative impulse is fundamentally recollective and other-directed, not decadent. The seductive present physicality of materialism gets refined, by time as by fire, in *The Spoils of Poynton*, and it becomes transmuted into memory, into a distant wail, into ghosts, into the imaginative impressions of the departed. Isabel, with all her advantages, stubbornly sits before blankness; Fleda Vetch becomes one upon whom nothing is lost.

And yet the book does not satisfy. The judgment of the crash of cinders, the igniting of canvasses, and the collapse of beams seems too severe for the innocent pleasures of the flesh—even those represented by the exquisite physicality of a Maltese cross. *The Spoils of Poynton* takes a heroine through grimmest purification and relinquishes not a moment of grace, not an ounce of relief, not a morsel of simple, soft, human sympathy. Fleda Vetch's negative path seems a brutal one. She looks at a nightmare of smoke, buries her face in her hands, and then seven minutes later she flees back to London and an ambiguous future, perhaps struck down by a mortal blow, probably a more vital woman. In *The Wings of the Dove* a wall more blank and pitiless than the consummation of Poynton will confront another heroine. Milly Theale, however, will take her hands away from her eyes, breathe the fragrance of grace, and attain victory over the essence of what, it would seem, the beautiful rival consistently represents.

5 "Via Negativa":
The Wings of the Dove

"Since I've lived all these years as if I were dead, I shall die, no doubt, as if I were alive—which will happen to be as you want me. So, you see," she wound up, "you'll never really know where I am. Except indeed when I'm gone; and then you'll only know where I'm not."

Milly Theale in *The Wings of the Dove*

One of the most powerful silences in James's fiction comes in *The Wings of the Dove*. Milly Theale is dying in Venice and Lord Mark sits gloomily in Florian's cafe after having announced the plot between Miss Croy and Mr. Densher. Milly discovers the plan to get her money and then turns to the wall, never, it would seem, to turn back. Yet she does turn back. She asks Sir Luke Strett to summon Densher to her *palazzo*. Kate Croy is kept out of the encounter in the private chamber—and so is the reader. Densher returns from Milly's palace and reports that "She had nothing to ask of me—nothing, that is but not to stay any longer. She did, to that extent, want to see me." Kate wonders that such a brief utterance could be the essence of the entire meeting. She asks, "And it took twenty minutes to make it?"[1] What transpires between Milly and Densher—forceful as wordlessness or as unreported words—provides one of the major structural silences of the novel.

Kate Croy herself seeks power through another structural silence which configures near the end of the novel, and she fails. The news eventually comes from the New York lawyers that Milly has named Densher as heir, but first a posthumous letter comes from the heiress herself. Densher offers it to Kate, with the seal unbroken, as a show of faith in their vow. She holds the letter, declares they both know it announces Milly's generosity, and then she tosses it into the fire. Again the text denies the reader—and Densher—immensely important information, and the silence which disturbs the reader obsesses Densher.

Then he took to himself at such hours, in other words, that
he should never, never know what had been in Milly's letter.
The intention announced in it he should but too probably
know; but that would have been, but for the depths of his
spirit, the least part of it. The part it missed forever was the
turn she would have given her act. That turn had possibilities
that, somehow, by wondering about them, his imagination
had extraordinarily filled out and refined. It had made of them
a revelation the loss of which was like the sight of a priceless
pearl cast before his eyes—his pledge given not to save it—
into the fathomless sea, or rather even it was like the sacrifice
of something sentient and throbbing, something that, for the
spiritual ear, might have been audible as a faint, far wail. This
was the sound that he cherished, when alone, in the stillness
of his rooms. He sought and guarded the stillness, so that it
might prevail there till the inevitable sounds of life, once more,
comparatively coarse and harsh, should smother and deaden
it—doubtless by the same process with which they would offi-
ciously heal the ache, in his soul, that was somehow one with
it. It deepened moreover the sacred hush that he couldn't
complain. [II, 429–30]

As the absence or stillness created by the destruction of Milly's letter
becomes first a cherished "far wail" and then a "sacred hush," a rarefied
silence develops as the dominant atmosphere of a novel where, when
the heroine disappears, she transforms into a more vital figure.

The Wings of the Dove builds upon increasingly evacuated centers,
which, like the ghosts of the tales, fascinate and preoccupy to the
exclusion of what might seem more healthy phenomena of life. Leon
Edel has said that "Merton Densher chooses to live with a ghost rather
than a strong and living woman,"[2] but that absented ghost itself has
grown to be strong and living, and as odd and perhaps as near to
sentimentality as this final twist may seem—and as close to morbidity—
it fulfills the irony working throughout the novel. Yet within a few
weeks of its publication, the characteristically negative novel dissatisfied
as perceptive a critic as Ford Madox Hueffer. When he asked James
why the reader was deprived of the "last interview" between Milly
Theale and Densher, the Master replied that the book was "composed
in a certain way, in order to come into being at all, and the lines of
composition, so to speak, determined and controlled its parts and

accounted for what is and isn't there."[3] Edel among others feels that the novelist plays with fire but does not want to get burned, so he leaves out such "great scenes."[4] Nonetheless, rather more intensity than less intensity is the result of the author's avowedly creative omissions.

The novel possesses signs of "absence par excellence" of the ghostly tales, but it has neither their feel nor their more sure morbidity. The universe expands to a much larger place in the novel, and what formerly may have sparked as splendid magic, here approaches—and never reaches—the transcendence of the religious consciousness. In his discussion of orthodoxy, G. K. Chesterton discriminates between unbalanced belief and true spiritual awakening. Chesterton notes that the madman's explanation is often complete, and, often, in a purely rational sense, satisfactory.

> Nevertheless he is wrong. But if we attempt to trace his error in exact terms, we shall not find it quite so easy as we had supposed. Perhaps the nearest we can get to expressing it is to say this: that his mind moves in a perfect but narrow circle; but, though it is quite as infinite, it is not so large. In the same way the insane explanation is quite as complete as the sane one, but it is not so large. A bullet is quite as round as the world, but it is not the world. There is such a thing as a narrow universality; there is such a thing as a small and cramped eternity.[5]

Chesterton's argument illuminates the narrowness of the ghostly tales in contrast to the greater universality of *The Wings of the Dove*. Preoccupations with worldly negation, moving along in progression—particularly in a tale like "Maud-Evelyn"—do lead to morbidity and suffocation in claustrophobic eternities, and what might have reached transcendence slides into the narrow crevice of obsession. However well-bred may be many of James's heroes and heroines, their passions often approximate the monomania of the governess of "The Turn of the Screw." They engage their anti-materialistic universe, not perhaps with all the marks of Chesterton's complaint, but with an unmistakable perceptual completeness troublesomely countered by decadent spiritual contraction.

The Wings of the Dove, however, brings negation closer to the arena of orthodox spirituality than to that of the occult, and, not surprisingly, the title provides broad reference to both biblical testaments. The painful constriction of "In the Cage"—telegraphic, mercantile, and suburban—gives way to the vague timelessness of a city dominated by a Byzantine temple, where beauty and decay intertwine. The "sacred hush" which Densher is unable to explain away distinguishes the novel's unworldly worldliness, and *The Wings of the Dove* explores a largeness of circle, in Chesterton's terms, which is found nowhere else in Henry James. It approaches questions which relate to James's unique incursion into formal philosophy, his 1910 "Is There a Life After Death?"[6] Eight years after the publication of *The Wings of the Dove* James obliquely but unequivocally asserts a belief in extended existences and a broadened field. He ends his discussion with the following passage.

> And when once such a mental relation of the question as that begins to hover and settle, who shall say over what field of experience, past and current, and what immensities of perception and yearning, it shall not spread the protection of its wings? No, no, no—I reach beyond the laboratory brain.[7]

The clinical brain of positivistic tradition finds explicit renunciation in this essay. In the novel the evanescent young heiress—little more than a shadow in life—finally spreads the protection of considerable spirituality over the materialistic plotting pair, but only after she meets the negation of death. Finally the young Englishwoman says, "I used to call her, in my stupidity—for want of anything else—a dove. Well, she stretched out her wings, and it was to *that* they reached. They cover us" (II, 438).

Nonetheless, the pregnant silences of the novel offer not only recreation, redemption, and sanctity. Death waits and compounds the novelist's difficulties. James faces the delicate task of subtly evoking the complexity of death's negation, a difficulty he himself indicates when in the "Preface" he writes that "This last fact was the real issue for the way grew straight from the moment one recognized that the poet essentially can't be concerned with the act of dying. Let him deal with the sickest of the sick, it is still by the act of living they appeal to him."[8] Much of the literature of death establishes opposition to life's abundance. There is life, full and rich, and then there is death and life is over—all offering the simplest correlative of death. That is as it should be in most cases, but Milly Theale dead is Milly Theale alive, and the artistic treatment must develop differently.

Her life does not stop and merely withdraw from the pitifully small degree of plenitude which seems her lot. The force of various voids, and of carefully developed absences, draws the reader who will never know what passed during the final interview with Milly, and who will never read the final letter she wrote. These silences and countless lesser silences place a tense emotional vacuum at the center of the novel's formal complexity. The sympathetic heiress finally merges with the structural silences which have been the emotional bases of the major scenes throughout.

Before investigating the subtlety of Milly Theale's quasi-religious venture, it is necessary to indicate the systematization with which the silences accumulate to build distinguished atmosphere and ultimately the vitality of her *via negativa*. The book begins with Kate Croy waiting for her father's entrance and soon presents the progress of the Croy line.

> . . . the whole history of the house had the effect of some fine, florid, voluminous phrase, say even a musical, that dropped first into words, into notes, without sense, and then, hanging unfinished, into no words, no notes at all. [I, 10]

The clutter of soundlessness contributes to the background tension from the start—"She hadn't given up yet, and the broken silence, if she was the last word, *would* end with a sort of meaning" (I, 6). Not simply providing the last word, but existing as it—and she will speak the last word at the end of the novel—Kate Croy initially is presented in an ambiguous relation to the silences which emerge as the surest expressions of Milly Theale. When she greets her father, her response to his claim of illness is "You're beautiful—*n'en parlons plus*" (I, 10). She asks that they speak of it no more, but the slight stated request for no words, although definitive, is made remote and abstract by the structural shift into the modality of another language. Tensions, energies and secrets move the text away from the distinctness of language.

After a splendid, indefinite introduction in Chapter I Lionel Croy disappears for good and re-enters oblivion to remain a handsome but quietly malevolent non-presence, but not before his daughter explains the unyielding silence her aunt demands in return for financial protection—"I shall have absolutely nothing to do with you; never see you, nor speak, nor write to you, never go near you nor make you a sign, nor hold any sort of communication with you. What she requires is that you shall simply cease to exist for me" (I, 17). Lionel Croy exists in the shadows, inexplicable—"He had always seemed—it was one of the marks of what they call the 'unspeakable' in him—to walk a little more on his toes, as if for jauntiness, in the presence of offense" (I, 18).

The shame of Kate Croy is her father's shame, "odious and vile" (I, 76) she calls it, and it is more potent because it is unnamed, as even her sister realizes.

> " 'Papa has done something wicked.' And the curious thing was that I believed it on the spot and have believed it ever since, though she could tell me nothing more—neither what was the wickedness, nor how she knew, nor what would happen to him, nor anything else about it. . . . We were not, however, to ask mother—which made it more natural still, and I said never a word. . . . No one has so much as breathed to me. That has been a part of the silence, the silence that surrounds him, the silence that, for the world, has washed him out. He doesn't exist for people." [I, 75–76]

Densher refuses to comprehend the bother about Lionel Croy—"You don't, you know, really tell me anything. It's so vague that what am I to think but that you may very well be mistaken? What has he done, if no one can name it?" (I, 77). Kate responds that "He has done everything." The positivists in Henry James, among them sane people like journalists Densher and Henrietta Stackpole, are loyal to apparent phenomena as the sum of the world. Densher's insensitive belief is that silence at best is vagueness and at worst superstition, not the oblique phenomenon which merits as much attention as more apparent communication.

The novel meticulously describes Merton Densher's education as it progresses from his first interview with Mrs. Lowder.

> It was an oddity of Mrs. Lowder's that her face in speech was like a lighted window at night, but that silence immediately drew the curtain. The occasion for reply allowed by her silence was never easy to take; yet she was still less easy to interrupt. The great glaze of her surface, at all events, gave her visitor no present help. [I, 92]

Slowly at first, Densher comes to appreciate implicit, unstated meanings.

> They sat for a little face to face upon it, and he was con-
> scious of something deeper still, of something she wished him
> to understand if he only would. . . . She said nothing—she
> kept that up. [I, 93]

The "keeping up" of silences, the maintaining of energetic reticence,
soon transforms the ominous silences which surrounded Lionel Croy
into an aspect of communication, although at this early stage relatively
little is communicated. Densher makes rapid progress in *The Wings of
the Dove* and abandons the habits of gross realism to develop a nascent
symbolist consciousness which allows him to approach an unworldly
spirituality and renounce worldly riches for what Fleda Vetch finally
perceived as her only just relic, "something sensibly gone."[9] In Chapter II
the atmosphere sustains itself "in silent sessions" (I, 35), and Mrs.
Lowder broaches the subject of Merton Densher after reference to Kate's
long silence—"I talk of him because you don't. . . . If I name that
person I suppose it's because I'm so afraid of him" (I, 43). And Mrs.
Lowder adds, "I dare say, I admit, that I shouldn't speak of him at all"
(I, 44). From the first, Kate Croy, "frequently soundless" (I, 6), keeps
silences that provide the tension of terror, and when Densher finally
appears, he emerges from that background.

Chapter III presents the encounter of Kate Croy and Densher at a
party, where they meet as across a metaphoric garden wall—"He could
say almost nothing to her—she scarce knew, at least, what he said. . . .
Never in life before had she so let herself go; for always before—so far
as small adventures could have been in question for her—there had
been, by vulgar measure, more to go upon" (I, 62–63). The pattern
re-asserts; the less there is to "go upon," with Lionel Croy, with Kate,
with Densher, with Maud Manningham, the greater the binding power.
These two people say nothing or say very little to each other and the
metaphorically separating gap—here the structure of the wall—defines
a motivating force in the relationship. Kate leaves Densher—"That
was one of the reflections made in our young woman's high retreat; she
smiled from her lookout, in the silence that was only the fact of hearing
irrelevant sounds, as she caught the truth that you could easily accept
people when you wanted them so to be delivered to you" (I, 64–65).
She withdraws from the passionate moment of first encounter and finds
that "Her intelligence sometimes kept her still—too still—but her want

of it was restless" (I, 66). Their relationship continues and they attain "periods of silence, side by side, perhaps even more, when a 'long engagement!' would have been the final reading of the signs on the part of a passer struck with them" (I, 66).

At the end of the chapter Kate Croy and Densher reunite in a distinguished moment.

> . . . Suddenly she said to him with extraordinary beauty: "I engage myself to you for ever."
>
> The beauty was in everything, and he could have separated nothing—couldn't have thought of her face as distinct from the whole joy. Yet her face had a new light. "And I pledge you—I call God to my witness!—every spark of my faith; I give you every drop of my life." That was all, for the moment, but it was enough, and it was almost as quiet as if it were nothing. [I, 106]

Talk, at its best, imitates quiet. No longer ambiguous sin, ominous opacity, or hinted communication, silence here uplifts the pair. Densher says he loves Kate and Kate's "answer to which was only the softness of her silence—a silence that looked out for them both at the far reach of their prospect" (I, 108).

This personification of their unspoken love looks out as quiet guardian—a figure which will evolve as the departed figure of Milly Theale. Before Densher and Kate part in Chapter IV, Densher assures his lover that Mrs. Lowder will keep silent concerning the pair's relation, and, with these remarks, Densher brings silence back to earth, back to associations of treachery. Then, as already reported, Kate informs Densher of her father's sin, talks of "the silence, the silence, that surrounds him, the silence that, for the world, has washed him out" (I, 76), and claims that Lionel Croy's silence is "a perpetual sound in my ears" (I, 80). At the end, Milly's unread letter will provide another major silence as sound, but here such a configuration begins to emerge.

By the end of Chapter VI all the significant characters have been introduced in relation to the unspoken. Then in Chapter VII Lord Mark arrives, the man who eventually breaks the matrix of silences to tell Milly that her two friends are engaged. He is the only player to speak clearly and offer definite words—although once again the text does not record them. Distinguished as a bloodless aristocrat, he speaks clearly and causes pain. Kate alone seems fooled by Lord Mark—and she misperceives many people. To her "he pointed to nothing; which was very possibly just a sign of his real cleverness, one of those that the really clever had in common with the really void" (I, 197). With the entry of Lord Mark—the dark *ficelle*—the stage is set.

At the end of Book Four, and throughout Book Five—the section which, in his "Preface," James called the heart of the novel, "the whole actual centre of the work"[10]—Milly Theale's adventure mildly begins.

> Milly had, under her comrade's eyes, a minute of mute detachment. She had lived with Kate Croy for several days in a state of intimacy as deep as it had been sudden, and they had clearly, in talk, in many directions, proceeded to various extremities. Yet it now came over her as in a clear cold way that there was a possible account of their relations in which the quantity her new friend had told her might have figured as small, as smallest, beside the quantity she hadn't. [I, 206–07]

In the same paragraph her first clear question concerning Densher emerges.

> It would have taken but another free moment to make her see abysses—since abysses were what she wanted—in the mere circumstance of his own silence, in New York, about his English friends. [I, 207]

Milly Theale experiences silent tension; the movement of the novel accelerates—"after the colloquy we have reported Milly saw Kate again without mentioning any name, her silence succeeded in passing muster with her as a new sort of fun" (I, 208–09). And what "happened was that afterwards, on separation, she wondered if the matter had not been mainly that she herself was so 'other,' too taken up with the unspoken; the strangest thing of all being, still subsequently, that when she asked herself how Kate could have failed to feel it she became conscious of her being here on the edge of a great darkness" (I, 210), and the images of the abyss and silence merge.

Book Four, Chapter V, ends with Milly and Susan discussing the possibility that Kate may indeed "care" for Mr. Densher, and Milly says, "If she did care Mrs. Condrip would have told me." Susan answers, "But did you ask her?" "Ah, no." "Oh!" said Susan. "Milly, however, easily explained that she wouldn't have asked her for the world" (I, 223). With this puzzling response the narration moves the conversation from quoted dialogue to indirect discourse. The shift reports the response without allowing the reader to "hear" the words, a structural shift which James often uses to approximate silences. At times Milly speaks important words; nevertheless, often at such moments the text withdraws from distinctness and draws speech toward a different modality, allowing utterance to merge with the unstated. The force of speech confuses with silence at critical moments. Milly Theale is one of James's most spiritual figures, and it is partly through such shifts from the more concrete phenomenology of spoken words to indirect report that her evanescent vitality develops. Definite artistic control uses degrees of remoteness, negation, and a background of a vaguely peopled void to build a correlative of the indefinite aura around a dying heroine. Eventually the tense inaccessibility merges with associations of grace.

With the advent of the Third Republic in France and with the loss of the Papal States to the Republic of Italy, the influence of the Catholic Church in Europe was clearly on the wane, and so it surprised many that in response to loss of influence the papal heart hardened into the infallibility doctrine of 1870. Yet while the church lost ground, it regained a nostalgic pull in those intellectual circles which most definitely had rejected her. Jean Pierrot carefully has traced the late and subtle shift back to Catholicism by members of the avant-garde—but not necessarily into orthodoxy. Mother Church became for them an almost purely aesthetic mistress, "a diffuse nostalgia for the supernatural already lurking in the background of some of their work."[11] Pierrot writes that:

> Faith has gone, artists seemed to be saying, yet we cannot be satisfied with a universe reduced solely to the interplay of purely material and physical forces. Faced with the sterility of the positivistic world, they proclaimed their belief in a supernatural universe, even though that belief remained rather vague and imprecise, largely because the intransigence of the Roman Church at first made any return to the relative certainty of traditional dogmas impossible. This is why the last two decades of the century saw the emergence of a whole gamut of trends that often, from the standpoint of Christian orthodoxy, are merely deviant products of a religious sensibility that is drawn

toward the supernatural while remaining incapable of finding
any solution to its need in any of the already-existing religions.[12]

Among those avant-garde writers who reconsidered the role of religion at *fin-de-siècle* was one of the closest friends James had made in
Paris, the French novelist and critic Paul Bourget (1852–1935). Early
in his career Bourget had distinguished himself with the publication of
the autobiographical verse novel *Edel* (1878), a work, it has been said,
which provided the first appearance in print of the decadent hero.[13]
And it was the more worldly Bourget who was responsible for having
James dine with Robert de Montesquiou, the aristocratic dandy upon
whom Huysmans in part modeled his Des Esseintes.[14] Yet despite his
early devotion to the refinement and morbidity of the decadent movement, Bourget was one of the first of the symbolist circle to reconcile
with some old ecclesiastical impulses. His 1883 *Essais de Psychologie
Contemporaine* broke ground by examining ignored trends in literature,
culture, and human psychology at century's end, and in it he made the
central point that a pervasive modern sadness brings man close to a
religious sensibility he can no longer accept.[15] Bourget explored Catholicism as aesthetic, purely as an aesthetic, and sought to find what might
be salvaged by the nonbeliever from its midst. He argued that in time
"faith will depart, but mysticism, even when expelled from the intelligence, will linger on in the sensations."[16] James himself called the
essais "almost brilliant," and when he met the author the next year
they had long talks. Yet for years James remained troubled by the
complex simplicity of Bourget's proposition. "Bourget est tragique,"
James wrote in a letter, "mais est-il sérieux?"[17]
Bourget was serious in his quasi-religious pronouncements and in
time his intensity would strain his friendship with James. Although as
late as 1895 James wrote that "Bourget's mind is, in the real isolation
in which I live, beneath what has been so much social chatter, a
flowering oasis in conversational sands," the year 1899 found Bourget's
impulses too narrow, too conservative, and perhaps too Catholic for
James's taste.[18] Yet Bourget's views were essential to the spirit of the
time. The dramatic critic Francisque Sarcey began to wonder at "the
unaccountable wind of mysticism blowing through France,"[19] while Max
Nordau decried the shade of the mystic dragged "into everything; into
magazines, both old and new; into newspapers, into poetry, the novel,
criticism, songs; into the theatre, into concerts; into the cafe-concert,

into revues, into specially written tragicomedies, into every genre you can think of."[20] And about the same time Camille Mauclair was commenting upon the glut of arcane religious imagery in the visual arts of the day.

> The salons bulged with Holy Women at the Sepulchre, Seas of Galilee, crucifixions, roads to Emmaus, pardons, and benedictions, all executed in the same bleached-out tones and with the same magic lantern lighting effects. . . . An appalling and unending plethora of missals, chausables, monstrances, and lilies. . . . All the external signs of faith were dragged in, and only faith itself was left out.[21]

Pierrot argues that it all began with Baudelaire's curious focus on women, woman as the merge of the sensual and the ascetic—"After all," Pierrot writes, "was the Baudelairean attitude to woman not a combination of quasi-religious worship and a sensual urge toward profanation?"[22] and indeed was not the same woman, in the view of Victor Charbonnel, one "who at the height of sensual ecstasy becomes a Christian divinity?"[23]

The Wings of the Dove is in part a product of these times, emerging as it does after James's movement through nascent and more mature symbolism, after his subsequent and scattered experiments with the impulses of decadence, and after the indistinct conflation of annihilation, purgation, and a Maltese cross in The Spoils of Poynton. It approaches fulfillment of Bourget's early reveries—the adaption of the religious aesthetic to the entirely secular consciousness. There may be many presences on the altars of the living and the dead in Henry James, but not one of them feels much like a deity. Nonetheless, the ultimately secular position of Milly Theale may owe much to the wave of mysticism which had swept Europe, and perhaps it owes something further to the "negative way" of some of the more disciplined mystical thinkers.

In April 1901, four months before Henry James began serious work on The Wings of the Dove, his brother arrived at Lamb House for an extended stay. During the five months of his visit, William wrote much of what he would soon deliver, at the University of Edinburgh, as the Gifford Lectures on "varieties of religious experience." To aid William's progress, Henry James offered the services of his own amanuensis, Miss Mary Weld, to type the versions of the lecture text. A few days after finishing her work on the lectures, Miss Weld began taking dictation on The Wings of the Dove.[24] In conversation, in draft, in composition, and in final published form, *Varieties of Religious Experience* was perhaps the work of his brother which Henry James knew on most intimate terms.

In his chapter on mysticism, William James presents an attack on what he considered the fakery of the more extremely occulated religious consciousnesses, and he aimed directly at John of the Cross, a "Spanish mystic who flourished—or rather existed, for there is little that suggested flourishing about him—in the sixteenth century."[25] While voicing disapproval, William James quoted extensively from *The Ascent of Mount Carmel*, the most well-known of the writings of John of the Cross.

> To know all things, learn to know nothing
> To possess all things, resolve to possess nothing
> To be all things, be willing to be nothing. . . .
> And if you attain to owing the All, you must own it,
>   desiring Nothing.
> In this spoliation, the soul finds its tranquility and rest.[26]

William James provides such evidence in his argument that John of the Cross betrayed "a vertigo of self-contradiction which is so dear to mysticism." When *The Wings of the Dove* appeared in 1902, William James read the novel with little sympathy, claiming that his brother had told no story and had "created a new *genre littéraire* which I cannot help thinking perverse."[27]

William James may indeed have found the novel somewhat perverse. It shows the extreme marks of a state which, in extremity, he rejected with considerable scorn.

> 1. *Ineffability.*—The handiest of the marks by which I classify a state of mind as mystical is negative. The subject of it immediately says that it defies expression, that no adequate report of its contents can be given in words. . . .
> 2. *Noetic quality.*—Although so similar to states of feeling, mystical states seem to those who experience them to be also states of knowledge. They are states of insight into depths of truth unplumbed by the discursive intellect. They are illuminations, revelations, full of significance and importance, all inarticulate though they remain; as a rule they carry with them a curious sense of authority for aftertime.

3. *Transiency.*—Mystical states cannot be sustained for long. Except in rare instances, half an hour, or at most an hour or two, seems to be the limit beyond which they fade into the light of the common day. Often, when faded, their quality can but imperfectly be reproduced in memory; but when they recur it is recognized; and from one recurrence to another it is susceptible of continuous development in what is felt as inner richness and importance.

4. *Passivity.*—Although the oncoming of mystical states may be facilitated by preliminary voluntary operations, as by fixing the attention, or going through certain bodily performances, or in other ways which manuals of mysticism prescribe; yet when the characteristic sort of consciousness once has set in, the mystic feels as if his own will were in abeyance, and indeed sometimes as if he were grasped and held by a superior power. . . . [28]

Here William James describes some of the most easily recognized elements of the late style of Henry James, with its passive renunciations, its flashes of enlightenment, its flood of unutterable perceptions. Max Beerbohm's parody of James in "A Mote in the Middle Distance," seems like nothing so much as an evanescent tissue of the ineffable, the noetic, the transient, and the passive.[29] They develop from such inarticulate epiphanies, as when Isabel Archer stands in a doorway and views her husband seated beside the standing Madame Merle, to profoundly deeper moments, such as when in front of a Bronzino portrait, for a transitory instant Milly Theale realizes, "I shall never be better than this." Such characters abandon themselves to curiously filled wordless moments which seem to transcend symbolist acuities and lead to the states of knowledge that William James finds central to the mystical impulse.

Bourget and his circle were not the only quasi-religious aesthetes who may have influenced James around the turn of the century. In the final chapter of *The Symbolist Movement in Literature* Arthur Symons presented his views on "Maeterlinck as Mystic" and argued for his unique importance in the arts—"The secret of things which is just beyond the most subtle words, the secret of expressive silences, has always been clearer to Maeterlinck than to most people"[30]—and for the guidance he offers to other dramatists. In *The Wings of the Dove* Milly's companion "knew her Maeterlinck" and the pair move around in a grand tableau that the narration reports recalled "some dim scene from a Maeterlinck play." James knew his Maeterlinck well, upon occasion had reviewed the Belgian author's work for the stage, and surely knew Symons's opinion of the dramatist.

> Maeterlinck has realized, better than any one else, the significance, in life and art, of mystery. He has realized how unsearchable is the darkness out of which we have just stepped, and the darkness into which we are about to pass. And he has realized how the thought and sense of that twofold darkness invade the little space of light in which, for a moment, we move; the depth to which they shadow our steps, even in the moment's partial escape. But in some of his plays he would seem to have apprehended this mystery as a thing merely or mainly terrifying; the actual physical darkness surrounding blind men, the actual physical approach of death as the intruder. . . . Here is mystery, which is also pure beauty, in these delicate approaches of intellectual pathos, in which suffering and death and error become transformed into something almost happy, so full is it of strange light.[31]

Milly Theale's story unfolds in the middle-ground between the vague, aesthetic mysticism of Maeterlinck's modern formulation—where "Souls are weighed in silence, as gold and silver are weighed in pure water, and the words which we pronounce have no meaning except through the silence in which they are bathed. We seek to know that we may learn not to know"[32]—and the inflexible rule of the medieval *via negativa*.

The suggestion cannot be proven, but it may be offered. Consciously or unconsciously Henry James of Rye 1901 may have assimilated some of the profound irony—if not the belief—of the spiritual seeker on the chill path of John of the Cross, where a stern deity dictates, "Learn to be empty of all things—interiorly and exteriorly—and you will behold that I am God."[33] John of the Cross recognized that certain spiritual consciousnesses might find vital spiritual awakening after a stern regime removed them from worldliness and the world. Denuded of appetites and even affections the soul would poise expectant, ready for the onrush of grace, the "dichosa ventura!" or "sheer grace!" of the *Noche Oscura*. But the dark night, rich with the poetics of negated promise, was a bleak descent into isolation, unrest, and suffering, and in his notes to the poem St. John writes that "it must be kept in mind that, as I explained before a person generally does not perceive this love in the beginning, but he experiences rather the dryness and the void we are speaking of."[34] The "passive purification" of the dark night, working on the intellect, the memory, and the will, finally prepares the spirit for marriage with Christ, but "few there are who walk along this road, because it is so narrow, dark, and terrible that, in obscurities and trials, the night of sense cannot be compared to it."[35]

The Wings of the Dove may partly transmute suffering, deprivation, and death into something luminous, but finally the difficult novel seems more fascinated with unyielding ironies—where negation and silence become plenitude and praise—than with the misty spiritual attenuations that fascinated many Continental sensibilities. Milly Theale grows increasingly silent and negative in her quest for the "life" that Sir Luke Strett names as her salvation. In time she begins to "enjoy boundless freedom, the freedom of the wind in the desert" that is early promised her. The image suggests a paradoxical freedom, absolute yet harsh and dry, and it relates to passages in the Gifford lectures that cite the text of John of the Cross:

> This is the peculiarity of the divine language. The more infused, intimate, spiritual, and supersensible it is, the more it exceeds the sense, both inner and outer, and imposes silence upon them. The soul then feels as if placed in a vast and profound silence, to which no created thing has access, in an immense and boundless desert, desert the more delicious the more solitary it is. There, in this abyss of wisdom, the soul grows by what it drinks from the well springs of the comprehension of love.[36]

The passage describes the freedom of James's heroine as she grows increasingly quiet and isolated in the novel, and it does so with words which repeatedly describe her condition—"silent," "solitary," "abysses," "exhilaration," and the empty but full freedom in a boundless desert. John of the Cross wrote that finally the pilgrim makes the ascent of the spiritual mountain and then ascends further—"There are souls who fly like birds which purify and clean themselves in the air."[37] The image approximates that of the wings of the dove.

Although Milly Theale's condition, as the heiress of the ages, suggests plenitude, it is her disinherited and negated state which distinguishes her. When she first appears in Book Third, she has stupendous wealth, but her positivity is specious. She is defined from the first in terms which oppose plenitude and which move along a negative path toward absences, silences, and voids—"It was New York mourning, it was New York hair, it was New York history, confused as yet, but multitudinous, of the loss of parents, brothers, sisters, almost every human appendage, all on a scale and with a sweep that required the greater stage" (I, 118). An oxymoronic relation of plenitude and loss emerges—loss so multitudinous that it needs the wide world for larger expression. William James said that the "handiest" mark of the mystical is the negative; something unworldly or even anti-worldly marks this heroine from the start. When her friend Mrs. Stringham reviews the opening scene, she begins "to recognise that an education in the occult— she could scarcely say what to call it—had begun the day she left New York with Mildred" (I, 116).

The artistic development of Milly Theale builds toward an ironic correlative, a full emptiness which reflects the Johannine metaphors; in death she gathers a near-mystical force and grows stronger than the living Kate Croy. The process develops along the lines of a structural archetectonic, laying foundations of vacancies, silences, negations— as distinguished energies—speechless moments, secrets, hidden disease, undiscovered sources of wealth, sin, or perception, broken sentences, unheard words, unseen letters, unexplained crimes, and perhaps most important, strong statements which offer impossibly remote opportunities for full explanation. When calm and silence finally climax in death, the accumulated dramatic silences merge and an absent force asserts itself. Some claim that Milly Theale grows luminous in contrast to the dark background[38]; yet it would seem that all else pales in relation to the vibrant emptiness she provides.

Early in the novel she foretold the end of her relationship with the Kensington crowd—" 'Since I've lived all these years as if I were dead, I shall die, no doubt, as if I were alive—which will happen to be as you want me. So you see,' she wound up, 'you'll never really know where I am. Except indeed when I'm gone; and then you'll only know where I'm not' " (I, 220). Such a seemingly overwrought fusion of contradictions, death as life, presence as absence, negation as affirmation, demonstrates not casual word play but marks of an artistically patterned spiritual awakening. As in those cases where the text shifts from direct to indirect discourse, the stylistic movement here approaches modalities of silence by shifting a passage of relative clarity into an expression of concentrated textual difficulty. The preceding reportorial function diminishes suddenly when Milly Theale comes forth with her gnomic declaration. Roland Barthes has spoken of the effect of trying to sort out the various shifts of language and the sometimes consequent dimming of voice which often seems the inevitable result of the pressure of difficulty. He writes that

> it is not violence which impresses pleasure; destruction does not interest it; what it desires is a place of loss, a fault, a break, a moment of deflation, the *fading* which seizes the reader at the moment of ectasy.[39]

The ecstasy of which Barthes speaks relates to Milly Theale's epiphany as she moves toward the "enigmas, gaps, and shifts" which Jonathan Culler has also identified as structurally developed sources of pleasure and value.[40]

The importance of metaphorical or literal lacunae is overwhelming in mystical literature. In *The Living Flame of Love* John of the Cross writes: "The day overflows into the day and the night teaches knowledge to the night. Thus one always calls to the other abyss [Psalm 41.8], that is: An abyss of light summons another abyss of light, and an abyss of darkness calls to another abyss of darkness, each evoking its like and communicating itself to it."[41] The primary image of full emptiness in *The Wings of the Dove* is the recurrent abyss which Milly Theale repeatedly confronts, as reiterative as John of the Cross's most catholic bottomless gulf—"the abyss of faith," "the abyss of wisdom," "the abyss of spiritual system," "the encircling abyss," "the abyss of the will," "the abyss of the ugly."[42] When Susan Stringham first discusses Kensington society, she tells Milly, "My dear child, we move in labyrinths." Milly replies, "Of course we do. That's the fun of it." Then she adds. "Don't tell me that—in this instance there are not abysses. I want abysses" (I, 206).

Peter Brooks suggests that the abyss in James "may be taken to stand for all the evacuated centers of meaning in his fiction that nonetheless animate lives, determining quests for meaning, and which confer on life, particularly on consciousness, the urgency and dramatics of melodrama."[43] Brooks's emphasis, on the genesis of that melodrama, may not lead to the mystical edge of John of the Cross, but his interpretation approaches, more than does that of any other critic, the *via negativa*. The bottomless abyss, a metaphorical focus of much mystical exploration, has little to do with the apparent schema of complications and complex relations. With the abyss, the patterns of gulfs, gaps, the

absent, the silent, and the voided assert themselves as primary confrontations. In Book Third Milly Theale entered the novel, sitting
before a physical and metaphysical abyss which extends as a paradox-
ically vibrant field.

> The whole place, with the descent of the path as a sequel to
> a sharp turn that was masked by rocks and shrubs, appeared
> to fall precipitously and to become a "view" pure and simple,
> a view of great extent and beauty, but thrown forward and
> vertiginous. Milly, with the promise of it from just above, had
> gone straight down to it, not stopping till it was all before her;
> and here, on what struck her friend as the dizzy edge of it, she
> was seated at ease. The path somehow took care of itself and
> its final business, but the girl's seat was a slab of rock at the
> end of a short promontory or excrescence that merely pointed
> off to the right into gulfs of air and that was so placed by good
> fortune, if not by the worst, as to be at last completely visible.
> For Mrs. Stringham stifled a cry on taking in what she believed
> to be the danger of such a perch for a mere maiden. [I, 137–
> 38]

Brooks has suggested as the novel's terminal image "Milton's invocation
of the Holy Spirit in Book I of *Paradise Lost*: 'Thou from the first/ Wast
present, and with mighty wings outspread/ Dove-like satst brooding on
the vast Abyss/ and mad'st it pregnant.' "[44] And Leon Edel has noted
the echo of the final words of Milton's epic poem—with the world "all
before her"—an echo he finds voiced on three occasions.[45] With an
allusion to Milton, the abyss suggests the challenging emptiness which
divine love faces before creation. Milly Theale confronts abysses, silences,
and emptiness; what is low she raises and supports. The allusion extends
the image's significance further and establishes a potentially powerful
heroine preparing to transform various voids through a negative way.
  The abyss may provide a dominant image in the novel, but the
moment in front of the Bronzino portrait provides the crucial scene—
"The whole actual centre of the work, resting on a misplaced pivot
and lodged in Book Fifth . . . " ("Preface," *The Wings of the Dove*),[46]
a moment which "served to Milly, then and afterwards, as a high water
mark of the imagination" (I, 230). The scene provides an explicit model
for the mystical modality defined by William James. Milly views the
lady of the painting and sees that with

her eyes of other days, her full lips, her long neck, her recorded
jewels, her brocaded and wasted reds, [she] was a very great
personage—only unaccompanied by a joy. And she was dead,
dead, dead. Milly recognized her exactly in words that had
nothing to do with her. "I shall never be better than this."
(I, 242)

The difficult passage ends with a linguistically troubling statement, the
construction of which suggests both the ineffability and the noetic
reversal of mystical experience. And it provides a substantial shift of
modality.

Culler writes of attempts to recuperate the text.

> The force, the power of any text, even the most unabashedly
> mimetic, lies in those moments which exceed our ability to
> categorize, which collide with our interpretive codes but never-
> theless seem right. Lear's "Pray you, undo this button; thank
> you, sir" is a gap, a shift in mode which leaves us with two
> edges and an abyss between them; Milly Theale's "pink dawn
> of an apotheosis" before the Bronzino portrait—"Milly rec-
> ognized her exactly in words that had nothing to do with her.
> 'I shall never be better than this.' "—is one of those interstices
> where there is a crossing of language and a sense that the text
> is escaping us in several directions at once. To define such
> moments, to speak of their force, would be to identify the
> codes that encounter resistance there and to delineate the gaps
> left by a shift in language.[47]

Although Culler makes no further comment on The Wings of the Dove,
his image of the linguistic abyss relates to the broad concerns of this
study. He speaks of the Bronzino scene, and of a related scene in King
Lear, where there is first the prelude of life and then the stroke of
death, repeated and repeated—incredibly in Lear with "Why should a
dog, a horse, a rat have life/ And thou no breath at all? Thou'lt come
no more/ Never, never, never, never, never"—and in The Wings of the
Dove with " . . . she was dead, dead, dead," until the strained language
breaks away from mimesis and approaches anti-language. Lear's request
for help comes after the blinding realization of Cordelia's death, Milly's
after a milder but related confrontation. Language builds force as it
approaches an abyss here, Culler's linguistic abyss, the abyss of death
which Milly Theale continually faces, perhaps the Johannine abyss of

negation. As Culler suggests, there appears in such scenes "one of those interstices where there is a crossing of language." In his most mystical work Maurice Maeterlinck spoke in words similar to Culler's, almost one hundred years before, when he wrote that "la présence, infinie, ténébreuse, hypocritement active de la mort remplit tous les interstices du poème"[48] [the infinite, dark, hypocritically active presence of death fills all the interstices of the poem]. For reasons that are linguistic, symbolic, and thematic, negations give force at such points in the text.

Language goes as far as it might in the face of experience of death. Lear's language shifts modes and drops many levels in an attempt to deal with expression at all, and the deepest effect comes no more from the meaning of Lear's words than from the distance between modalities, between what is said and what *has* been said—"Never, never, never, never, never./ Pray you, undo this button." With sure clarity for detail Milly sees the rich surface of a life which might reflect her own; she then points at the condition in which she finds herself—most certainly not at the picture on the wall, as Lord Mark believes—and her focus leaps from the utterly specific to the exciting vagueness which has troubled many readers. The intense ambiguity here is one of the most important structural approaches to silence.

The words Milly Theale finally speaks come from the other side of the world from those of the recorded details. The ambiguous antecedent of the word "this" at the end of her pronouncement causes fierce difficulty, but the entire matrix of her words, and the narration leading to them, works for related structural ambiguity. There rises the large problem of making clear the statement that she "recognized her exactly" and then denying with "nothing." Is it that the words had nothing to do with her? Or does the emphasis fall on *that* (i.e., the thing itself) had nothing to do with her? Then there are the double possibilities of the two references to "her," leading to eight possible combinations of meaning due to antecedential shift—first *her*, the lady of the Bronzino, second *her*, Milly; first *her*, Milly, second *her*, Milly again; first *her*, Milly, second *her*, the lady of the Bronzino; etc. The sense of "recognized her exactly in words" is certainly remote, and the report that these words had nothing to do with her seems to imply, as final effect, an antithesis to words. The whole statement and the implication of the noetic antithesis to language produces verbalization informed with the tension, conflict, contradiction, and negation of mystical vitality.

After she views the Bronzino, Milly Theale moves further along on a *via negativa*. In the next scene "there was the moment at which she almost dropped the form of stating, of explaining, and threw herself, without violence, only with a supreme pointless quaver that had turned, the next instant, to an intensity of interrogative stillness, upon his [Sir Luke's] good will" (I, 253). William James had written somewhat scornfully of the encounter "in mystical literature [of] such self-contradictory phrases as 'dazzling obscurity,' 'whispering silence,' 'teeming desert,' which are continually met."[49] Milly Theale's vibrant silent stance and her freedom, that of the wind in the desert, express characteristic associations of the mystical state which flowers in contradictory phrases—from Milly's "intensity of interrogative stillness," to Milly "intensely motionless" and "intensely still," to her "charged stillness," to her growing perception of "remarks that were really quite soundless," to the numerous movements when "things were understood without saying, so that he could catch in her, as she but too freely could in him, innumerable signs of it, the whole soft breath of consciousness meeting and promoting consciousness."[50]

Still in the hall where she viewed the painting, Milly draws Kate Croy aside and makes her first dramatic request—"Will you render me to-morrow a great service?" Her friend says that she will, "Any service, dear child, in the world." Milly then asks for her company on a visit to the renowned London physician, Sir Luke Strett—" 'I thought,' Milly said, 'you would like to help me. But I must ask you please, for the promise of absolute silence' " (I, 247–49). The scene ends in this attenuated moment of sworn secrecy, all the more charged because it shares the ambiguous energy gathered in front of the Bronzino portrait.

Then Milly makes a second visit to the physician's examination room "far back in the fine old house, soundless from position," and the intensely waiting atmosphere is maintained in a room where "she thought of all the clean truths, unfringed, unfingered, that the listening stillness, strained into pauses and waits, would again and again, for years have kept distinct" (I, 259). Science abandons empiricism in *The Wings of the Dove* and this excellent medical man offers clairvoyance. The examination is sufficiently brief that Kate Croy wonders, "But could he in so few minutes ask you enough—?" Milly answers, "He asked me scarcely anything—he doesn't need to do anything so stupid" (I, 254). Physician becomes priest in a ceremonial chamber; he tells Milly "to 'live.' " Milly appreciates his advice as compassionate, "but its operation for herself was as directly divesting, denuding, exposing" (I, 277). Then she takes her sole excursion alone, a seemingly negative journey, and it enlivens her.

. . . in spite of the fact, as that would help the requirements of adventure, her way was exactly what she wanted not to know. . . . This was the real thing; the real thing was to be quite away from the pompous roads. . . . There was a sort of spell in the sense that nobody in the world knew where she was. It was the first time in her life that this had happened; somebody, everybody appeared to have known before, at every instant of it, where she was; so that she was now suddenly able to put it to herself that that hadn't been a life. [I, 273–74]

More alone than ever, under a "sort of spell" of isolation, she makes her solitary way. Sir Luke had "wished her also, it was true, not to make, as she was perhaps doing now, too much of her isolation" (I, 274), but her life here approaches an engaged experience of that isolation, as it rejects the companionship, the fine companionship, which she determines had not been life. Alone for the first time, she approaches "adventure." Away from the labyrinths, she "looked for a bench that was empty, eschewing a still emptier chair that she was hard by and for which she would have paid, with superiority, a fee" (I, 274). This strange, slightly ominous line may recall the scene before the Bronzino, but in this "extraordinary hour" (I, 275), Milly Theale feels life as it would seem she has never felt it before.

An acutely ironic perception invigorates the void here in what might be perceived as an instance of noetic revelation. Susan Sontag has examined similar occurrences and has suggested that "perhaps the quality of attention one brings on something will be better (less contaminated, less distracted) the less one is offered. Furnished with impoverished art, purged by silence, one might then be able to transcend the frustrating selectivity of attention. . . . A stare is perhaps as far from history, as close to eternity, as contemporary art can get."[51] Sontag's reference is perceptual, not mystical; nonetheless, the denudation of worldly phenomena—the goal and end of the *via negativa*—and the intense concentration of perception lead her to the concerns of transcendence and the eternal, and they carry artistic discipline to the portal of the other-worldly. In such a scene James approaches Bourget's project—the pulse of occult force, unaccompanied by belief. Milly Theale entered the world of London life to find the "greater stage" and enrich her experience, but life eluded her there. On the distant grass, in the "empty" chair, the young woman sits as she first sat before the abyss in the mountains—and as she will finally turn alone to face the wall. The structures of silence and of fecundated voids are reiterative bases here. She marks the human condition of her melancholy comrades and with the ironic tension of holding herself "intensely motionless" (I, 275), Milly Theale begins to uncover life.

Such moments of vital isolation are near the end of the *via negativa* of John of the Cross.

> The small white dove
> Has returned to the ark with an olive
> And now the turtledove
> Has found its longed-for mate
> By the green river banks.
>
> She lived in solitude
> And now in solitude has built her nest;
> And in solitude He guides her,
> He alone, Who also bears
> In solitude the wound of love.[52]

Milly's isolation deepens in Venice, where under the shadow of the Byzantine cathedral the odor of decay merges with the fragrance of grace. In her grand *palazzo* the dying "Milly moved slowly to and fro as the priestess of worship," and increasingly the metaphors of the spiritual seeker apply to her. "Certainly it came from the sweet taste of solitude, caught again and cherished for the hour; always a need of her nature, moreover, when things spoke to her with penetration. It was mostly in stillness that they spoke to her best . . . amid voices she lost the sense" (II, 149). The metaphors move the aesthetic toward a more persistent orientation.

> She made now, alone, the full circuit of the place, noble and peaceful while the summer sea, stirring here and there a curtain or an outer blind, breathed into its veiled spaces. She had a vision of clinging to it; that perhaps Eugenio could manage. She was *in* it, as in the ark of her deluge, and filled with such a tenderness for it that why shouldn't this, in common mercy, be warrant enough? She would never, never leave it—she would engage to that; would ask nothing more than to sit tight and float on and on. The beauty and intensity, the real

momentary relief of this conceit, reached their climax in the positive purpose. [II, 157]

The passage presents the emphatic negative image of a woman clinging to silences, the quiet and seemingly empty veiled spaces, and finding in this conceit positivity. She would "engage to that," and the sense of "engage" recollects the marriage she might have had with Densher. Milly Theale, on the negative path, makes her life by engaging the experience of the abyss which throughout the novel presents itself as part of her peculiar birthright.

Only after returning from the park does Milly begin consciously to understand the irony which rules her life; the negative comes round as the positive way.

> Directness, however evaded, would be, fully, for *her*; nothing in fact would ever have been for her so direct as the evasion. Kate had remained in the window, very handsome and upright, the outer dark framing in a highly favorable way her summery simplicities and lightnesses of dress. Milly had, given the relation of space, no real fear she had heard in their talk; she hovered there as with conscious eyes and some added advantage. . . . It seemed to pass between them, in fine, without a word, that he was in London, that he was perhaps only round the corner; and surely therefore no dealing of Milly's with her would yet have been so direct. [I, 297–98]

The relation of Milly Theale to spatial imagery changes; before, she perched at the edge of the alpine cliff, here she "hovers" above the "relation of space." In the scene direct knowledge passes wordlessly.

Sitting beside Lord Mark she remembers the confrontation of the "Bronzino [as] the climax of her fortune." This crucial scene, perhaps the most extreme expression of full negation, demands lengthy quotation. Here the antitheses of life, at least the superficial antitheses of life as phenomena, unequivocally are asserted.

> She couldn't have said what it was, in the conditions, that renewed the whole solemnity, but by the end of twenty minutes a kind of wistful hush had fallen upon them, as if before something poignant in which her visitor also participated. That was nothing, verily, but the perfection of the charm—

or nothing, rather, but their excluded, disinherited state in the presence of it. The charm turned on them a face that was cold in its beauty, of a possible but forbidden life. It all rolled afresh over Milly: "Oh, the impossible romance—!" The romance for her, yet once more, would be to sit there for ever, through all her time, as in a fortress; and the idea became an image of never going down, of remaining aloft in the divine, dustless air, where she would hear but the plash of water against the stone. The great floor on which they moved was at an altitude, and this promoted the rueful fancy. "Ah, not to go down—never, never to go down!" she strangely sighed to her friend.

"But why shouldn't you," he asked, "with the tremendous old staircase in your court? There ought of course always be people at top and bottom, in Veronese costumes, to watch you do it."

She shook her head both lightly and mournfully enough at his not understanding. "Not even for the people in Veronese costumes. I mean the positive beauty is that one needn't go down. I don't move in fact," she added—"now. I've not been out, you know. I stay up. That's how you happily found me."

Lord Mark wondered—he was, oh yes, adequately human. "You don't go about?"

She looked over the place, the storey above the apartments in which she had received him, the *sala* corresponding to the *sala* below and fronting the great canal with its gothic arches. The casements between arches were open, the ledge of the balcony broad, the sweep of the canal, so overhung, admirable, and the flutter towards them of the loose white curtain an invitation to she scarce could have said what. But there was no mystery, after a moment; she had never felt so invited to anything as to make that, and only that, just where she was, her adventure. It would be—to this it kept coming back—the adventure of not stirring. "I go about just here." [II, 162–63]

She finds the perfection of "positive" beauty in her "excluded and disinherited state," and she rejects the splendid people in Veronese costumes to attain the "adventure of not stirring" as the adventure of her life. No handsome journalist rests at the heart of Milly Theale's vitality. The reader understands such fulfillment because the structural development of the novel has all along worked to inform the quiet and the void with complex tension and energy.

Sitting up in her *palazzo*, motionless on her idiosyncratic *via negativa* and deciding never to go down, Milly Theale tells Lord Mark, " 'I've the best advice in the world. I'm acting on it now. . . . ' She finally spoke as if for amusement; now that she had uttered her truth, that he had learnt it from herself as no one had yet done, her emotion had, by the fact, dried up. There she was; but it was as if she would never speak again" (II, 171). In spite of the strong sense of life she finds on the negative path, it is part of the characteristic pattern that her vital emotion diminishes when she speaks, positively, of it.

Some readers may find the discoveries of Milly Theale and John of the Cross terrifying—death in life becomes life. They are terrifying. Yet no matter how removed from "life" Milly Theale may be, she grows increasingly *engagé* in, actually "engaged to," her removed condition. Perhaps Kate Croy comes closest to the truth. She tells Densher that Milly Theale was "satisfied" and had "realised her passion. She wanted nothing more. She had *all* she wanted" (II, 360–61). There is no soft optimism here. At the emptiest of moments, Milly Theale turns to the blankness of the wall and feels the negative passion of life in a high, ironic reverse vision—perhaps the supreme ironic development of Henry James—which is as "cold in its beauty" as the figure in the Bronzino portrait. The novel expresses a capacity to experience life, stubbornly and resiliently, in spite of major obstacles and pitiless negations, and for this reason it is both a humanistic work and a spiritual one. Yet it never crosses the quavering line of religious belief, and the artistic achievement never allows the book's anti-phenomenological bias to solidify into code or theology.

The Wings of the Dove ends with perfect poise. Nonetheless no clear salvation falls to Densher and Kate Croy, for the arduous journey still lies ahead of them—a journey which seems to begin with the rejection of materialism which is the first step of a *via negativa*. No simple grace pursues Milly Theale's death, and readers who speak of her pure *caritas* and her transcendent love may read more kinesis into her spirituality than should be read. She expires in the delicate fragrance of grace, but her position is supremely precarious. A few months later "The Beast in the Jungle" will close with the confrontation of hellish pessimism, after a man engages himself to a similar species of energetic void.

In 1902 Milly Theale contemplates the abyss and makes it pregnant; in 1903 John Marcher's abyss matures as a viciously overgrown field of emptiness. It may seem strange to compare the dying heiress and the empty man, but surely his adventure evolves as nothing more nor less than the "adventure of not stirring," which, it seems, was Milly Theale's apotheosis. The symbolist chamber, darkening, promising and limited, particularly fascinated the painters Khnopff, Klinger, and Mellery, and it was a safe stage set which, in the words of Robert Goldwater, was "shrouded in a mysterious continuum, in which a not too solid matter shades imperceptibly into a space not truly void, both informed by the same silent spirit, a spirit which can be overheard in silence."[53] But in James these fascinations eventually move from cautious metaphorical interiors into the hostility of an aggressive world where reversals startle. The full emptiness of *The Wings of the Dove* shifts one step into the empty fulness of John Marcher's jungle, into the redundant image of a hostile and mindlessly vegetative undergrowth which completely denies the aesthetic clarity of Johannine stoicism.

Milly Theale is not John Marcher—her negations ruthlessly drive at her from without, his from within. Nonetheless it may seem to the reader that she "finds life" just by the good fortune of a hair and at moments by mystical sleight of hand. The aesthetic bravado of *The Wings of the Dove*, one which so boldly denies the facts of the flesh that the heroine promises never to smell of medicine or of the sickroom, confronts an unsympathetic and bestial naturalism in "The Beast in the Jungle." Sufficient differences exist between these two disinherited people that the sky parts to accept one while the dark woods rush up to claim the other, but they attain to a similarly isolated revelry of stillness.

Milly Theale's love does not surely cleanse her of the taint of perverse fascination with her own life's morbidity. Marcher loves himself, but Milly Theale bequeaths a stupendous fortune to Densher; and yet, as proof of vital love, such materialistic dross seems a dim emblem of spiritual devotion—unless the dying girl means the gift with full irony. The powerful vacancies of the novel, as correlatives of undefinable spiritual presences, would seem to condense into a cold affair in the heap of gold. In fact the inheritance seems more the discard of final denudation than it does the inspired gift of all-informing love. Perhaps the revelation of the destroyed letter would demonstrate her deep devotion to the shallow man, but at the end the tower of gold uneasily dominates the horizon. The destroyed letter may work for the correlative of Densher's loss, but it does little to underscore the force of Milly's profound affection. Indeed, this annihilation may have been one of the few metaphorical silences in Henry James which fail to create the intended life.

The young heiress moving through her soundless *palazzo* does not signify perfection. Yet it seems clear, at least to this reader, that James intended no compromise to his heroine's integrity. Nonetheless, Milly Theale does not descend from a flawless line of ancestors. Over twenty years before, in *Washington Square*, another mild-mannered young heir-ess was pursued by a splendid young man who found her somewhat dull. The young women in both tales finally comprehend the suitors' false courtships. Milly then dies, but Catherine Sloper retreats to the near-death of a twenty-year seclusion. Both turn to the wall and both come to terms with the vitality of similar silences and similar voids. Catherine Sloper is in fact the first Jamesian heroine to comprehend, vaguely, that seeming vacuities in life can richly inform human expe-rience; indeed, beside them flesh and blood at times may seem insignificant.

Morris Townsend walked out of her life, and for twenty years his name was unspoken in her house. He was the singular subject which neither she nor her aunt introduced. Then what happens happens suddenly. Townsend re-enters her parlor, still with "a very fine presence, and a fair and lustrous beard, spreading itself upon a well-presented chest, [which] contributed to its effect." He stands beside her in the most revelatory moment in the work.

> Catherine still said nothing, and he may well have recalled with apprehension her ancient faculty of silence. She contin-ued to look at him, however, and as she did so she made the strangest observation. It seemed to be he, and yet not he; it was the man who had been everything, and yet this person was nothing. How long ago it was—how old she had grown—how much she had lived! She had lived on something that was connected with *him*, and she had consumed it in doing so. This person did not look unhappy. He was fair and well-preserved, perfectly dressed, mature and complete.[54]

An antithesis develops in the way that Catherine Sloper deeply has felt the experience of life. The man whom she faces, whom she once loved, shifts into equation with nothingness, and, "complete," he stands before her as lifeless absence. The *impression* of his loss, however, developed as the motivating force in this middle-aged woman's life.

She tells Townsend, "Impressions last, when they are strong. But I can't talk." The major reversal takes place, and the positive presence of Morris Townsend pales beside the overwhelming potency of his absence.

Finally he asks why she never married, for she did have opportunities.

> "I didn't wish to marry."
> "Yes, you are rich, you are free; you had nothing to gain."
> "I had nothing to gain," said Catherine. [WS, p. 265]

As a supreme positivist, Townsend speaks of materialism, but Catherine, a woman who does not easily accustom herself to falsehood, echoes his words to speak of something entirely different. In "The Art of Fiction" James wrote that, "If experience consists of impressions, it may be said that impressions *are* experience." Catherine Sloper has lived, at least according to the essay's critical formulation. The impressions of her life—primary ones of emptiness and the dramatic lacuna left by Townsend's flight—defined, matured, and eventually exhausted her.

Catherine Sloper and Milly Theale concentrate on harsh deprivations. It is the saddening, perhaps slim truth that what they miss forms the basis of what they win. Yet in 1881 James provided little affirmation for such stubborn vitality. When the romantic suitor returns, the structural gap finally closes, the drama completes, the twenty-year silence breaks, and suddenly a woman's life shrivels to the point of a knitting needle, to a morsel of fancywork, to the dot of present phenomena which closure evacuates of vitality. Both New York heiresses find a sort of life in a negative way, but the cruelty of *Washington Square* seems overwhelming; perhaps this is part of the reason why Henry James excluded the novella from his commemorative New York Edition. In *The Wings of the Dove* the sickly girl can claim the aesthetic dignity of death's extreme negation. The integrity of her silences is maintained and sealed. Yet there can remain only partial confidence that she sustains ironic vitality during all the days which dwindle, unmarked in the text, until her death.

If James intended the enlightenment of *The Wings of the Dove* as an apologia for the extraordinarily quiet life, at times he must have had grave doubts. For extended moments Catherine Sloper and John Marcher both share the passions of Milly Theale, and both meet frigid ends. Milly Theale is saved by the controlled associations of an extreme ascetic impulse and of quasi-mysticism, although she never approaches the leap of faith fundamental to the Johannine way. However struck James may have been by whatever he knew of the mystical poetics, his work provides a *via negativa* which remains an uneasily poised aesthetic, an exquisitely rarefied stoicism, rather than anything pointing to the clear confidence of transcendence.

Milly Theale triumphs over Kate Croy, and this triumph is the first instance in James of the negative way's successful assertion over the positive seduction of the world. *Roderick Hudson*'s Mary Garland, so patient a Griselda—perhaps too significantly a Mary from a New England town called Nazareth—adopts a mature discipline in *The Wings of the Dove*. The rule brings vitality and a victory of a sort, and yet the optimism here derives from an agony of imaginative reconsideration which hardly can be offered as readily accessible. Milly Theale may spread her wings, but she does so because of intense control which prevents her from flinching. At the grimmest of moments she turns to the blankness of the wall and feels the passion of life in a high ironic reverse vision. Hers is the revelation of an aestheticized stoicism which some might call perverse or decadent, and the revelation does not surely satisfy. In spite of the unquestionable vibrancy of this strange masterpiece, the image of the wings of the dove ultimately remains as overwhelmingly fragile as it is beautiful. It will be another American heroine, quiet and retired, but distinguished by a newly evolved resilience, who will only seemingly choose the negative way—but who will gain back the world.

6 "Via Positiva": The Golden Bowl

"Do not wonder that I know all languages since I know what men do not say."

Apollonius of Tyana

Although it is a long novel written in a complex late style, *The Golden Bowl* makes a definitive retreat from the word. The narration takes long explorations, tensions hover for pages, interior monologue and even interior dialogue distinguish the prose, but gone is the patter of repartee and the effortless swell of speech. When spoken dialogue comes, it comes strained and constricted and it moves hesitantly, as talk which approaches silence.

Two distinct silences inform Maggie Verver's slightly spiritual education, that which is mute, passive, and empty, and that which communicates with force. The book traces subtle ironies in a cunning *vita activa* as Maggie Verver matures and discovers that the silences which were a prison invigorate and liberate her. She moves toward enlightened silence and at times her development is not entirely unlike that of Hamlet. She discovers horrors in beds, betrayals within family, foul incest of a modern sort, and she is paralyzed terribly. Like Hamlet she must act, but she must not act; she must speak, but she must not speak. The characters Henry James creates in the late novels populate a horrifically balanced universe where people struggle for an order which they intensely must work to maintain. A false move might collapse the delicate structure and spin all into chaos. Utterance might break the symmetry, widen the surface fault—therefore Maggie Verver maintains vigilant wordlessness. The tormented Prince of Denmark was trapped into silence or into the near-silence of wordplay. Finally he speaks and speaks rather plainly; Ophelia falls into madness and the stage becomes cluttered with bodies.

As a modern and as a Jamesian, however, the Princess works to avoid the blood-splattered stage. She acts as forcefully as Hamlet eventually does, although her major concern is not vengeance. She learns that purposeful action may be non-action and that the wordplay which saves may be silence. As George Steiner has stated, silence need not be passivity.

> . . . there are actions of the spirit rooted in silence. It is difficult to *speak* of these, for how should speech justly convey the shape and vitality of silence? But I can cite examples of what I mean.
>
> In certain Oriental metaphysics, in Buddhism and Taoism, the soul is envisioned as ascending from the gross impediments of material, through domains of insight that can be rendered by lofty and precise language, toward ever deepening silence.[1]

Although Steiner presents the problem any critic might face who risks tracing "the shape and vitality of silence," he states that the "primacy of the word, of that which can be spoken and communicated in discourse, is characteristic of the Greek and Judaic genius and carried over into Christianity."[2] The quasi-mysticism of *The Wings of the Dove* brought James to the furthest edge of a Graeco-Judaic linguistic primacy and removed his dying heroine to a hermetic lingering, far from her Byzantine city's rich redundancy. Steiner's consideration of the vitality of silence abandons the central positivity of Christian *logos* in favor of an oriental metaphysic; it is this metaphor which provides an unusual focus for considering the difficulties of *The Golden Bowl*.

Few might confidently label Henry James an orientalist, and yet the striking pagoda image that opens Book Second is clearly an oriental one. Particularly disturbing in the heart of London, the structure has puzzled many readers, most of whom consider it a romantic image revealing the immaturity of Maggie Verver. Yet the shift from Christian capital to the Far East seems to involve no romantic assertion of personal force or expression. Something alien to the boisterous energy of London appears at the heart of the matter and recalls Maeterlinck's belief that the Orient and the Occident are mutually impenetrable and eternally foreign to one and another.

This situation had been occupying, for months and months,
the very centre of the garden of her life, but it had reared
itself there like some strange, tall tower of ivory, or perhaps
rather some wonderful, beautiful, but outlandish pagoda, a
structure plated with hard, bright porcelain, coloured and figured and adorned, at the overhanging eaves, with silver bells
that tinkled, ever so charmingly, when stirred by chance airs.
She had walked round and round it—that was what she felt;
she had carried on her existence in the space left her for
circulation, a space that sometimes seemed ample and sometimes narrow: looking up, all the while, at the fair structure
that spread itself so amply and rose so high, but never quite
making out, as yet, where she might have entered had she
wished. She had not wished till now—such was the odd case;
and what was doubtless equally odd, besides, was that, though
her raised eyes seemed to distinguish places that must serve,
from within, and especially far aloft, as apertures and outlooks,
no door appeared to give access from her convenient garden
level. The great decorated surface had remained consistently
impenetrable and inscrutable.[3]

The pagoda provides a balanced but complex surface, rigid on four
sides, probably representing the stance of Charlotte, Amerigo, Adam,
and Maggie herself. It suggests some of the negative energy of alien
terror and the required silence of contained secrets.

> . . . a Mahometan mosque, with which no base heretic could
> take liberty; there so hung about it the vision of one's putting
> off one's shoes to enter, and even, verily, of one's paying with
> one's life if found there as an interloper. [II, 4]

Whether mosque or temple or pagoda—James characteristically treats
the metaphor with considerable latitude—implications emerge of discipline, initiation, study, and belief.

The novel began with the aristocratic Italian liking his London.

> If it was a question of an *Imperium*, he said to himself, and if
> one wished, as a Roman, to recover a little the sense of that,
> the place to do so was on London Bridge, or even, on a fine
> afternoon in May, at Hyde Park Corner. [I, 3]

Book First begins in the milieu of shouting Hyde Park orators, the fullness of empire; Book Second opens with Maggie Verver confronting an entirely different metaphor, one unyielding and enigmatic in its suggestion of withheld but easily asserted power. The leap of faith from civilization's barren richness to the fecund sterility of an Eastern symbolism rests at the base of a persistent Anglo-American poetic tradition. In *Four Quartets*, "Burnt Norton," T. S. Eliot evokes the force of tense restraint in Oriental art.

> Words move, music moves
> Only in time; but that which is only living
> Can only die. Words, after speech, reach
> Into the silence. Only by the form, the pattern,
> Can words or music reach
> The stillness, as a Chinese jar still
> Moves perpetually in its stillness.[4]

Chinese jar or pagoda or mosque, the oriental images suggest the concurrence of complete stillness and full energy. The quality belongs to much of Eastern art; in Western thought it rarely finds successful expression, except, perhaps, in Dante's whirlwind of heavenly order or in the resolution of a baroque fugue. Yet even in such cases the balance is swung and the effect is more of attaining stillness through perpetual movement rather than reaching full vitality through unbroken stillness.

Wittgenstein later would explore the relationship between word and fact and would call that relationship frighteningly weak. In *The Golden Bowl* the speakers' words are generally irrelevant to what is transpiring. They are useful more because they keep up the veil at critical moments, but almost nothing of real value receives report through speech. Maggie Verver's progress would seem to support the view proposed by Maeterlinck twenty years before Wittgenstein that "It is idle to think that, by means of words, any real communication can pass from one man to another."[5]

From the first, language delivers coarse commodities in the novel, and those characters, like Bob Assingham, who ask easy questions and easily provide answers, receive severe reprimand.

> His wife had once told him, in relation to his violence of
> speech, that such excesses, on his part, made her think of a

retired General whom she had once seen playing with toy
soldiers, fighting and winning battles, carrying on sieges and
annihilating enemies with little fortresses of wood and little
armies of tin. . . . It was natural, it was delightful—the romance, and for her as well, of camp life and of the perpetual
booming of guns. It was fighting to the end, to the death, but
no one was ever killed. [I, 66]

The predominant talk in the novel is the talk of these two people,
mostly ridiculous with their ridiculous names. They talk all the time.
It is their only occupation. Their constant gabbling in the background
does provide the reader with necessary information in this so silent
book, but the Assinghams emerge as no more than undignified com-
mentators with clicking mandibles, soon to be left behind, gossiping
in the halls, as Maggie Verver quietly moves to center stage. Nonetheless, despite their lack of weight, a basic choral function seems
clear—although this function seems considerably less explicit than it
might be in, strikingly, Sophocles' *Antigone*, where according to May
Daniels, the "silence remains, as it were, in the background; it is not
brought forward, made the main interest of the play and allowed to
speak for itself. It is left to Chorus and Messenger explicitly to comment
on its nature and significance."[6]
     Despite a constantly diminishing perspective, this observant husband
and wife provide dialogue which, at least in Book First, explains some
of the interweaving ironies of speech and silence. Fanny knows more
about such matters than does Bob—perhaps because of the Eastern
heritage she hints at when she stares from under her "lids of Jerusalem"
(I, 36). Referring to the issues at hand and the items at stake, Fanny
Assingham proclaims:

> " . . . It *is* always the Prince, and it is always, thank heaven,
> marriage. And these are the things, God grant, that it will
> always be. That I could help, a year ago, most assuredly made
> me happy, and it will continue to make me happy."
>   "Then why aren't you quiet?"
>   "I *am* quiet," said Fanny Assingham.
>   He looked at her, with his colourless candour, still in his
> place; she moved about again, a little, emphasising by her
> unrest her declaration of her tranquillity. [I, 84]

The book traces a growing awareness of reversals: what seems active is often passive, and what appears passivity evolves as fullest activity.

From the point when Charlotte Stant and Amerigo enter the Bloomsbury shop, the force of all significant action is exerted through silences.

> The man in the little shop in which, well after this, they lingered longest, the small but interesting dealer in the Bloomsbury street who was remarkable for an insistence not importunate, inasmuch as it was mainly mute, but singularly, intensely coercive. . . . He was clearly the master, and devoted to his business—the essence of which, in his conception, might precisely have been this particular secret that he possessed for worrying the customer so little that it fairly made for their relations a sort of solemnity. [I, 108]

His selection of goods is complimented in terms of verbal spareness— "He had not many things, none of the redundancy of 'rot' they had elsewhere seen" (I, 109). In a slightly dusty corner of Bloomsbury a moderately guilty couple meets a very quiet little man. He establishes the subsequent tone and introduces an uneasy note—"Then the shopman, for Charlotte, momentously broke silence. 'You've seen, disgraziatamente, signora principessa,' he sadly said, 'too much'—and it made the Prince face about" (I, 115).

Ironically, a glutting takes place in the spare shop, and odd conversation begins. Charlotte and Amerigo "had between them often in talk the refrain, jocosely, descriptively applied, of 'old Roman' " (I, 114). The concept of refrain suggests what begins to develop. Speech is extremely constricted between important characters in the novel. Whenever intensely delicate issues are being discussed or, more accurately, when they are being touched upon, the dialogue hesitates. When Charlotte tells Amerigo she could not show Maggie any token received from the Prince, he asks, "Why in the world not?"

> "Because—on our basis—it would be impossible to give her an account of the pretext."
> "The pretext—?" He wondered.
> "The occasion. This ramble that we shall have had together and that we're not to speak of."

> "Oh yes," he said after a moment—" I remember we're not
> to speak of it." [I, 114–15]

These lines provide an early but characteristic example of the incremental progress of communication in the novel, the catching onto the
previously spoken words, the slight addition to them, the turn of a
corner, and here at least, the end in an asserted silence. The rhythms
of refrain, control, and some repetition develop.

In Eliot's movement toward faith, struggling up the purgatorial
mountain toward the "word unheard" of Four Quartets, he passes through
many stages. In "Ash Wednesday" an agonizing religious poet gropes
with fragmentary utterances which might extend his religious experience. The poem offers two variants on the tradition of the Roman
Litany of Our Lady. The first more calm and orderly:

> Lady of silences
> Calm and distressed
> Torn and most whole
> Rose of memory
> Rose of forgetfulness
> Exhausted and life-giving[7]

From a long way off the poet looks toward some aspect of silent perfection. But the other variant offers the sound of a litany as a more
fragmented attempt to make words express what must remain
inexpressible.

> Although I do not hope to turn again
> Although I do not hope
> Although I do not hope to turn

At dramatic moments in The Golden Bowl the dialogue explores rhythms,
structures, and sometimes vocabularies which echo religious incantation. When, oppressed by the quiet of the shop, the Prince rejects the
golden bowl, both he and Charlotte feel intense strain.

> "But it's exquisite," Charlotte, as if with an interest in it
> now made even tenderer and stranger, found herself moved
> to insist.
> "Of course it's exquisite. That's the danger."

. . . "The danger—I see—is because you're superstitious."
"Per Dio, I'm superstitious! A crack is a crack—and an omen's an omen."
"You'd be afraid—?"
"Per Bacco!"
"For your happiness?"
"For my happiness."
"For your safety?"
"For my safety."
She just paused. "For your marriage?"
"For my marriage. For everything." [I, 123–24]

The pressure of reality and of sensible danger here restricts the spoken word. What the insecure friends communicate under the surface of their speech hints at peril—the subject is their sexual future.

Repeatedly, at crucial moments in The Golden Bowl, litanic, constricted patterns of chant-like speech recur, and the patterns often share the sense of Eliot's religious gropings. Whenever characters approach vows of silence, as Amerigo and Charlotte do here, their speech tightens. Immediately before Maggie Verver takes her final plunge into silence, in fact renouncing further conversation with Fanny Assingham on the subject of Amerigo's adultery, she participates in one of the novel's grandest litanic echoes. She tells Fanny Assingham she will work her will in silence, never making a sound.

"My dear child, you're amazing."
"Amazing—?"
"You're terrible."
Maggie thoughtfully shook her head. "No I'm not terrible, and you don't think so. I do strike you as surprising, no doubt—but surprisingly mild. Because don't you see—I am mild. I can bear anything."
"Oh, 'bear'!" Mrs. Assingham fluted.
"For love," said the Princess.
Fanny hesitated. "Of your father?"
"For love," Maggie repeated.
It kept her friend watching. "Of your husband?"
"For love," Maggie said again. [II, 120]

Scattered, fragmented speech is one thing, but something substantially different develops in *The Golden Bowl*. As a modernist, James knows the limitations of the word, but he does not move in the direction of the absurdist theater, where meaningless speech chokes human expression and human vitality. On the contrary, James works against deafness and mutism. Steiner has written of related concerns:

> The crisis of poetic means, as we now know it, began in the later nineteenth century. It arose from awareness of the gap between the new sense of psychological reality and old modes of rhetorical and poetic statement. In order to articulate the wealth of consciousness opened to the modern sensibility, a number of poets sought to break out of the traditional confines of syntax and definition. Rimbaud, Lautréamont, and Mallarmé strove to restore to language a fluid, provisional character; they hoped to give back to the world the power of incantation—which it possesses when it is still a form of magic.[8]

May Daniels has observed that, in the theater of Maeterlinck, "the vague sense of anguish emerges in a dreamy iterative dialogue, wandering repetitions of half thought, echoing and dying." This she sees in response to a "primitive naked fear" which overwhelms many of the characters in the plays. Daniels speaks of the hypnotic effect, at times incantatory, on the nerves of the spectator, as the Maeterlinckian dialogues gather the "power of haunting music." It is, perhaps, notable that Fanny Assingham "fluted" her response to Maggie's echoing response. Certainly Debussy saw the potential of such moments when he wrote *Pelléas et Melisande*, his haunting opera on one of Maeterlinck's most suggestive texts. But the hypnotic effect persists in most of Maeterlinck's works, and, throughout, the meaning of the words is far less significant than the rhythms and echoes of utterance.

MALEINE.	Mais cependant . . . je vois la mer.
LA NOURRICE.	Vous voyez la mer?
MALEINE.	Qui,oui, c'est la mer! Elle est verte!
LA NOURRICE.	Mais alors, vous devez voir la ville. Laissez-moi regarder.
MALEINE.	Je vois le phare.
LA NOURRICE.	Vous voyez le phare?

MALEINE.	Qui. Je crois que c'est le phare . . .
LA NOURRICE.	Mais alors, vous devez voir la ville.
MALEINE.	Je ne vois pas la ville.
LA NOURRICE.	Vous ne voyez pas la ville?
MALEINE.	Je ne vois pas la ville.[9]

Maeterlinck, however, does not often provide "the wealth of consciousness opened to the modern sensibility" of which Steiner speaks. On the contrary, his characters verbally stagger under the weight of their particular terrors, and their "incantation" comes closer to the stuttering of a Wozzeck than it does to a restored language of power. Indeed Daniels argues that in such passages we find what "might have been extracted from an infant's reading book."[10] Even Maeterlinck himself was not insensible to "beaucoup de naïvetés dangereuses . . . ces répétitions étonnées qui donnent aux personnages l'apparence de somnambules un peu sourds constamment arrachés à un songe pénible" [a great deal of dangerous naivety . . . these astonishing repetitions which give to the characters the aspect of sleepwalkers who are constantly being drawn through a painful dream].[11]

James's iterative dialogues, however, do reveal higher levels of consciousness, and the broken talk sounds far less like stuttering. The spoken words present a progress, from person to person, which echoes the structural forms of ecclesiastical antiphones and shares their resonance. The distance to benediction or liturgical silence is not always great. Steiner's provisional quality emerges as the Jamesian dialogue drives toward incantation and then, upon occasion, into the inspiration of silences. The few words spoken chant out solemnity and add primitive power to the speech of these ultra-sophisticated people. The effect approaches the related "magical and evocative poetry" of which Mario Praz speaks.[12] When Maggie Verver and Fanny Assingham grapple over the horrors which they see too clearly, they are as halting as druids under the full moon. Naomi Lebowitz accurately speaks of Maggie as "priestess/princess,"[13] for in time the liturgical associations grow strong.

Bernard P. Dauenhauer has noted that at times of stress and crisis, Catholic liturgy reverses its normal progress from ritual austerity to richness, its normal movement, in the words of liturgical historian Anton Baumstark, "from simplicity and brevity towards greater richness and prolixity."[14] Liturgical reforms, under pressure of inner and outer threat, "tend to simplify formulas and gestures and to reintroduce silent spaces into the flow of the liturgical act."[15] In a related manner James them to it. Ritualistic speech asserts the importance of limited speech as James transforms the language he retains.

Clearly here the ritualistic language seems fundamentally alien to the incantation of Praz's magical romanticism, a sensibility which seems closer to dream inexpression than to tense denial of utterance. Silence and near-silence in *The Golden Bowl* function to delimit and control rather than to produce mystical expansiveness. They work to control fear. The "mastertone" of much symbolist theater, particularly that of Maeterlinck, has been called that of terror,[16] and such terror rises consistently in the novel. Stephen Spender recognized the profound uneasiness of *The Golden Bowl* and perceived the idiosyncratic development of a "technical mastery which has the perfection of frightful balance and frightful tension."[17] In the prefaces he wrote for the New York Edition, James offered well-known remarks on the nature of terror as it evolved throughout his fiction.

> Really, universally, relations stop nowhere, and the exquisite problem of an artist is eternally but to draw, by a geometry of his own, the circle within which they shall happily *appear* to do so. He is in the perpetual predicament that the continuity of things is the whole matter, for him, of comedy and tragedy; that this continuity is never broken, and that, to do anything at all, he has at once intensely to consult and intensely to ignore it. All of which will perhaps pass but for a supersubtle way of pointing the plain moral that a young embroiderer on the canvas of life soon began to work in *terror*, fairly, of the vast expanse of surface, of the boundless number of its distinct perforations for the needle, and of the tendency inherent in his many-coloured flowers and figures to cover and consume as many as possible of the little holes.[18]

The Golden Bowl explores more than Maggie Verver's initiation into evil. It offers her rebirth into the devastating complexity of experience, of vast surfaces, of ramification and complication. Terror, so defined, and evil might be worlds apart. She tells the Prince of her expectations: " 'I shall see wonders, I know. I've already seen them, and I'm prepared for them,' Maggie recalled—she had memories enough. 'It's terrible'— her memories prompted her to speak" (II, 357). Initially accepting the integrity of the surface, Maggie Verver awakens to a devastating world where experience never stops. J. A. Ward marvels at the number of relations between people in the novel: the Assinghams say, "There's Maggie's and the Prince's, and there's the Prince's and Charlotte's . . . there's Charlotte's and the Prince's . . . there's Maggie's and Charlotte's and there's also Maggie's and mine. I think that there's Charlotte's and mine."[19] Yet Ward shows how incomplete even these tabulations are and points to nuances and transformations that extend the relations out boundlessly. Maggie faces a heaving reality in *The Golden Bowl* as she explores an interrelatedness which frequently verges on the chaos that Spender saw James confronting in a foreboding of World War I horrors.

The electric arena of *The Golden Bowl*, poised on the brink of collapse, is held in place by the ruling intelligence, in this case Maggie Verver's, and symmetry and silence develop as the conservative artistic tools which she employs. Behind the walls of the pagoda, below the elegant surfaces, rest grim configurations, and Maggie fears that any

> alteration of his [Amerigo's] consciousness, even in the possible sense of enlivenment, would make their precious equilibrium waver. *That* was at the bottom of her mind, that their equilibrium was everything, and that it was practically precarious, a matter of a hair's breadth for the loss of the balance. It was the equilibrium, or at all events her conscious fear about it, that had brought her heart into her mouth; and the same fear was, on either side, in the silent look she and Amerigo had exchanged. [II, 17–18]

Maggie then considers speaking to her husband about the superiority of their relationship, but something holds her back.

> Some such words as those were what *didn't* ring out, yet it was as if even the unuttered sound had been quenched here in its own quaver. It was where utterance would have broken down by its very weight if he had let it get so far. [II, 19]

Doubts of her husband's faithfulness must be kept, at the very least, from her father, and the resolute, absolute silence seems the unbearable instrument of her confinement—"To say anything at all would be, in fine, to have to say *why* she was jealous; and she could, in her private hours, but stare long with suffused eyes, at that impossibility" (II, 36).

Yet she continues positing some kind of statement, until finally she understands that her wordlessness itself begins to exert pressure on Charlotte and Amerigo.

> They had had to read into this small and all-but-suppressed variation a mute comment—on they didn't quite know what; and it now arched over the Princess's head like a vault of bold span that important communication between them on the subject couldn't have failed of being immediate. [II, 43]

In response Charlotte and Amerigo keep up their silence.

> They had built her in with their purpose—which was why, above her, a vault seemed more heavily to arch; so that she sat there in the solid chamber of her helplessness, as in a bath of benevolence artfully prepared for her, over the brim of which she could but just manage to see by stretching her neck. . . . She had flapped her little wings as a symbol of desired flight, not merely as a plea for a more gilded cage and an extra allowance of lumps of sugar. Above all she hadn't complained, not by the quaver of a syllable. [II, 45]

The metaphoric prisons of chambers, vaulted ceilings, gilded cages, and threatening pagodas initially express the control Maggie Verver must maintain in face of a suspicion. But while waiting for the right words to come, she retires into impotence.

> Day after day she put off the moment of "speaking," as she inwardly and very comprehensively, called it—speaking, that is, to her father; and all the more that she was ridden by a strange suspense at his himself breaking silence. [II, 50]

In time she feels less trapped by the silences and begins to decipher them; she finally understands the Prince's reticence as his clearest admission of guilt at Matcham. And because her father says nothing concerning the pair's weekend away, Maggie suspects that he suspects too.

> Finally, at the end of April, she decided that if he should say nothing for another period of twenty-four hours she must take

it as showing that they were, in her private phraseology, lost.
[II, 50]

The strain continues to build.

> It was in their silence that the others loomed, as she felt; she
> had had no measure, she afterwards knew, of this duration,
> but it drew out and out—really to what would have been called
> in simpler conditions awkwardness—as if she herself were
> stretching the cord. [II, 56–57]

But the words which might wrong the affairs fail to come.

> Touch by touch she thus dropped into her husband's silence
> the truth about his good nature and good manners. . . . It
> would be a question but of the most trival act of surrender,
> the vibration of a nerve, the mere movement of a muscle; but
> the act grew important between them just through her doing
> perceptively nothing. . . . "Come away with me, somewhere,
> you—then we needn't think, we needn't even talk, of any-
> thing, of anyone else:" five words like that would answer her,
> would break her utterly down. But they were the only ones
> that would so serve. She waited for them, and there was a
> supreme instant when, by the testimony of all the rest of him,
> she seemed to feel them in his heart and on his lips; only they
> didn't sound. [II, 62–63]

Waiting for such words, Maggie experiences increasing pain in her
progressive awareness. Her stillnesses with Amerigo evolve into communication, rough at first, initially not unlike the assertions of Bob
Assingham's military language—"They had silences, at last, that were
almost crudities of mutual resistance—silences that persisted" (II, 63).
At the end of Chapter 27, still early in the long section named for
her, for the last time the Princess tries to use inevitably halting speech
to escape her stifled condition. She breaks silence.

Maggie wants Charlotte alone so that she might, perhaps, suggest
her own fears and perhaps talk her rival into a corner. To clear the
stage she asks that Amerigo "agreeably" invite Adam off on a vacation,
but the "precautionary" Prince understands that such a request—
apparently odd considering the blissful symmetry of the foursome—

might need to be strongly made. Maggie is struck by her husband's suggestion of possible harm—"With their stillness together so perfect, what had suggested so, around them, the attitude of sparing them?" The Prince's opposition asserts itself.

> "So that unless I insist—?"
> "We shall simply go on as we are."
> "Well, we're going on beautifully," he answered—though by no means with the effect it would have had if their mute transaction, that of attempted capture and achieved escape, had not taken place. [II, 68]

Capture. Through incremental linguistic shifting the Prince continues to turn conversation in a direction which must deeply disturb his wife. He then suggests that *Charlotte* suggest the excursion to Adam, thereby, Maggie realizes, giving an indelicate or daring Charlotte the option to make the situation or to break it. Amerigo suggests that Charlotte might push the point by saying that Maggie herself was "above all concerned for the proposal." Charlotte, he says, will "be able to tell him the reason" (II, 68).

Maggie comprehends how the ramification of words, like experience, "never stops," and the consequent terror she experiences allows the Prince's escape. Maggie loses the verbal battle and the Prince goes on to play his last card: "That I think it would be so charming. That we've persuaded *her* will be convincing." "I see," says Maggie (II, 69). Increasingly in these early chapters language provides a loose web, however tightly Maggie attempts to hold on. Spoken words—civilized, controlled, modulated and carefully planned—almost send her world into catastrophe. In the coach with her husband she finds herself far worse off than when she began the conversation.

> It was almost as if, having planned for the last word, she saw him himself enjoying it. It was almost as if—the strangest way in the world—he were paying her back, by the production of a small pang, that of new uneasiness, for the way she had slipped from him during their drive. [II, 69]

Maggie abandons faith in speech and begins the next chapter with a "new uneasiness." She understands that her talk has given Charlotte and Amerigo a dangerous advantage—they might now mention to Adam Verver the oddity of his daughter's request.

> She recognised by the end of the week that if she had been in a manner caught up her father had been not less so—with the effect of her husband's and his wife's closing in, together, round them, and of their all having suddenly begun, as a party of four, to lead a life gregarious, and from that reason almost hilarious, so far as the easy sound of it went, as never before. [II, 70]

In *The Golden Bowl* the reiterated metaphors of heard and unheard noise, of sound and of screams, express the cumulative charge of increasing terror and decreasing control. Powerless to speak to Amerigo, Maggie cannot confront Charlotte, and she sees the impossibility of approaching her father.

> For how could she say as much as that without saying a great deal more? without saying "They'll do everything in the world that suits us, save only one thing—prescribe a line for us that will make them separate." How could she so much as imagine herself even faintly murmuring that without putting into his mouth the very words that would have made her quail? [II, 76]

She cannot try the Prince again—"She couldn't challenge him, because it would have been—and there she was paralysed—the *note*. It would have translated itself on the spot, for his ear, into jealousy; and, from reverberation to repercussion, would reach her father's exactly in the form of a cry piercing the stillness of peaceful sleep" (II, 79). By this point silence offers Maggie only some grace as she and her father move "slowly through large still spaces; they could be silent together, at any time, beautifully, with much more comfort than hurriedly expressive. It appeared indeed to have become true that their common appeal measured itself, for vividness, just by this economy of sound" (II, 80).

She demonstrates an appreciation of silence's expressiveness when she visits Fanny Assingham, the sole remaining person to whom she can speak of her pain—"I'm saying that I'm bewildered, tormented, and that I've no one but you to speak to."

"And if I'm both helpless *and* tormented I stuff my pocket-handkerchief into my mouth, I keep it there, for the most part, night and day, so as not to be heard too indecently moaning. Only now, with you, at last, I can't keep it longer; I've pulled it out, and here I am fairly screaming at you. . . . I go about on tiptoe, I watch for every sound, I feel every breath, and yet I try all the while to seem as smooth as old satin dyed rose-colour." [II, 114–15]

In this chapter she reveals the full extent of her helplessness, and yet she shows more signs of a growing acuteness.

"Their least danger, they know, is in going on with all the things that I've seemed to accept and that I've given no indi-cation, at any moment, of not accepting. Everything that has come up for them has come up, in an extraordinary manner, without my having by a sound or a sign given myself away— so that it's all as wonderful as you may conceive. They move at any rate among the dangers I speak of—between that of their doing too much and that of their not having any longer the confidence or the nerve, or whatever you call it, to do enough." Her tone, by this time, might have shown a strange-ness to match her smile; which was still more marked as she wound up. "And that's how I make them do what I like!" [II, 119–20]

"You're terrible," responds Fanny Assingham. Maggie will maintain surface passivity, and she will thereby separate Charlotte and Amerigo. She takes her stand and then before departing she holds Mrs. Assingham in a wordless embrace which will reassert itself, with insistence, as one of the book's significant gestures.

Dorothea Krook notes the unusual arrangements in *The Golden Bowl*.

When the golden bowl is broken, the Prince in the subsequent scene does indeed learn that his wife Maggie knows "every-thing." But immediately after that the silence is resumed; and in the critical period that follows at Fawns, Mr Verver's country-house, Maggie speaks never another word about it to the Prince, the Prince speaks never a word to Charlotte, Charlotte never a word either to the Prince or Maggie, and none of them, of course, utters a syllable to Adam Verver who knows (or appears to know) nothing whatever about the whole matter from the beginning to the end of the story.[20]

Krook goes on to say that Maggie's silence is the "firmest abstention from pressure," an attempt, "by not insisting, by not pressing or harassing her husband the Prince, but, instead, simply letting him alone— to [let Amerigo] see for himself the shamefulness of his act of betrayal, to come by his own effort to the knowledge of good and evil."[21]

Although Maggie's silence does allow the Prince some freedom to read his own guilt and thereby grow morally, one might further argue that Maggie increasingly applies subtle pressure. The metaphors which populate the book, of military battle, of capture and escape, of caging and imprisonment, of Charlotte finally raging as a screaming cat held by the silver cord of Adam's opaque wordlessness, all counter the idea that the central silences of the book provide withdrawal from pressure. Krook emphasizes the wordlessness of a passive woman who, in her view, might view the Prince and "silently suffer with him and watch over him in his anguish as he struggles to come to his knowledge of good and evil."[22] Carl Maves seems to imply a more active silence when he speaks of a growing concern of "the heroism of inaction"[23] in the Major Phase, and indeed that passive activity of Maggie Verver seems crucial.

When Maggie confronts her husband with the barest facts of the golden bowl, she applies the pressure of a Renaissance instrument of torture, and she knows it. If she said a bit more, he would know where he stood and what he felt.

> But this was exactly the door Maggie wouldn't open to him; on all of which she was the next morning asking herself if, thus warned and embarrassed, he were not fairly writhing in his pain. He writhed, on that hypothesis, some seconds more, for it was not till then that he had chosen between what he could do and what he couldn't. [II, 200]

Maggie told Fanny Assingham that she would make them do what she liked by a silence that superficially seemed passivity, but which would allow for control—"She was having, by that idiom, the time of her life—she knew it by the perpetual throb of this sense of possession, which was almost too violent either to recognise or hide" (II, 212).

"Learning, almost from minute to minute, to be a mistress of the shades" (II, 147), when Maggie next appears before Fanny Assingham, she is anything but passive in her stillness.

> Yet there was some knowledge that, exactly to this support of her not breaking down, she desired, she required, possession of; and, with the sinister rise and fall of lightning unaccompanied by thunder, it played before Mrs. Assingham's eyes that she herself should have, at whatever risk or whatever cost, to supply her with the stuff of her need. [II, 164]

Lightning unaccompanied by thunder, reminiscent of Kawabata's claim for an Eastern "silence like thunder," suggests the controlled but intense pressure of the maturing heroine. The few words with which she continues to address her husband do not offer him relief; they evolve as the cold, quaverless utterance of report, cheerful and cheerless fulfillments of daily duties, but they have nothing to do with the powerful issues at hand. She tells her friend:

> "Oh, I don't know that I shall speak—if he doesn't. But his keeping away from me because of that—what will that *be* but to speak? He can't say more or do more. It won't be for me to speak," Maggie added in a different tone, one of the tones that had already so penetrated her guest. "It will be for me to listen." [II, 173]

By maintaining an essential silence concerning what she suspects or knows, and concerning what Adam Verver knows, by leaving her husband with the impossible and tormenting injunction—"Find out for yourself!" (II, 211)—Maggie Verver moves toward stronger control— "as hard, at this time, in spite of her fever, as a little pointed diamond, the Princess showed something of the glitter of consciously possessing the constructive, the creative hand" (II, 150–51). Fanny Assingham predicted that Maggie would partly work her will through silence, and that Charlotte and Amerigo would remain "mystified, confounded, tormented. But they won't *know*—and all their possible putting their heads together won't make them. That . . . will be their punishment" (II, 141). Susan Sontag has said that "a person who becomes silent becomes opaque for the other; somebody's silence opens up an array of possibilities for interpreting that silence, for inputing speech to it," and "this opaqueness induces spiritual vertigo."[24] Everyone feels the pressure of the silence which Maggie choreographs, and as Fanny states:

> "One's punishment is in what one feels, and what will make ours effective is that we *shall* feel." She was splendid with her "ours"; she flared up with this prophecy. "It will be Maggie herself who will mete it out."
> "Maggie—?"
> "*She'll* know—about her father; everything. Everything," she repeated. On the vision of which, each time, Mrs. Assingham, as with the presentiment of an odd despair, turned away from it. "But she'll never tell us." [II, 141]

In the end no one knows what Maggie knows, and her almost entirely unspeaking father helps. He emerges at the end as "quiet, patient, exquisite," perhaps "sublimer even than Maggie herself" (II, 140).

Charlotte proves the unequal opponent and her terminal image is presented consistently. She rattles in the halls, screams in the corridors, chatters to the guests. Her method of control has been verbal; she asks Maggie to name names and at one point seems to dare Maggie to name her. Confident of her ability to manipulate words, she attempts to force Maggie to speak. Insufficiently understanding Maggie's power to grasp the imagination and stir terror, Charlotte loses the scene. At the end Amerigo will damn her with what seems a terrible curse—"She's stupid," he says. The brilliant polyglot, Charlotte sinks into utter passivity at the end—kept in line by the wordless collaboration of the Ververs. Adam and his young wife roam around the estate at the end:

> . . . and the likeness of their connection would not have been wrongly figured if he had been thought of as holding in one of his pocketed hands the end of a long silken halter looped around her beautiful neck. He didn't twitch it, yet it was there; he didn't drag her, but she came; and those indications that I have described the Princess as finding extraordinary in him were two or three mute facial intimations which his wife's presence didn't prevent his addressing his daughter. . . . They amounted perhaps only to a wordless, wordless smile, but the smile was the soft shake of the twisted silken rope, and Maggie's translation of it, held in her breast till she got well away, came out only, as if it might have been overheard, when some door

was closed behind her. . . . "but she's afraid to ask, don't you
see? just as she's afraid of not asking; just as she's afraid of so
many other things that she sees multiplied round her now as
portents and betrayals." [II, 295–96]

Charlotte's final position seems like that which, in May Daniel's words,
defines Maeterlinck's pathetic "mute Cassandra, petrified with fear,
'trembling like a wild beast in a snare.' "[25]
     Maggie tells no one of the embrace that Charlotte gave her or that
she gave Charlotte because the event "had taken on perceptibly the
special shade of consecration conferred by unanimities of silence" (II,
284); the cumulative silences excite the quartet with "some occult
power" (II, 286). Maggie and her father find the company of the house
"weakening the emphasis of so many of the silences of which their
intimate intercourse would otherwise have consisted," but Charlotte is
presented in loud metaphor—"Her voice, high and clear and a little
hard, reached her husband and her stepdaughter while she thus placed
beyond doubt her cheerful submission to duty. Her words, addressed
to the largest publicity, rang for some minutes through the place,
everyone as quiet to listen as if it had been a church ablaze with tapers"
(II, 299).

> So the high voice quavered, aiming truly at effects far over
> the heads of gaping neighbours; so the speaker, piling it up,
> sticking at nothing, as less interested judges might have said,
> seemed to justify the faith with which she was honoured.
> Maggie, meanwhile, at the window, knew the strangest thing
> to be happening: she had turned suddenly to crying, or was
> at least on the point of it—the lighted square before her all
> blurred and dim. The high voice went on; its quaver was
> doubtless for conscious ears only, but there were verily thirty
> seconds during which it sounded, for our young woman, like
> the shriek of a soul in pain. [II, 300]

Although, inevitably, some words are involved in Maggie's manip-
ulations, speech ultimately functions differently for her than it does for
Charlotte. At first Maggie attempted to use speech, as Charlotte consistently does, to destroy the silences. From Chapter 31 on she uses
spoken words to maintain and intensify them, to build idiosyncratic
power, and one-by-one to draw friends and family into wordlessness.

Under extreme pressure, in a place "vivid in its stillness" (II, 252), Charlotte falters, and in a garden presented as a "brilliant void", (II, 316) she confronts her rival. Throughout the ensuing scene Maggie dictates the action, as she had planned to do—"They might have been figures rehearsing some play of which she herself was the author" (II, 242).

"Is there any wrong you consider I've done you?" (II, 254), Charlotte asks. By denying any wrong—thereby essentially offering her friend a structure of silence—Maggie ends Charlotte's move toward power. Her opacity had applied the pressure which literally forced her imaginative rival's outbreak; then her strongest possible denial leaves Charlotte no out-routes and quiets her absolutely—"I've never thought of you but as beautiful, wonderful and good. Which is all, I think, that you can possibly ask" (II, 258). Charlotte, with her fatal flaw, "held her a moment longer: she needed—not then to have appeared only tactless— the last word" (II, 258). Charlotte asks that Maggie swear on her honor, and so Maggie does. The oath seals Charlotte's fate. Charlotte, who has been a superb battler with words, can ask no more, cannot draw from Maggie the slightest further utterance which might be turned back against her.

The positivistic rival, early in James linked to materialism and more apparent phenomena, here operates in the more subtle positivity of language. The only honor, merit, goodness, and, most importantly, control she can maintain is of surface reality and speech. She must accept the supposed validity of those surfaces, and of Maggie's assertion, or she must relinquish her foundation. Ruth Yeazell writes that Charlotte's "is a dream which finally may be only a matter of words, not genuine feelings, but it nonetheless holds out to us a consoling possibility." Yeazell argues that, "Confronting Charlotte for the last time, Maggie thus allows her to assert—and perhaps half-believe—that returning to America has been all her own idea"[26]

Charlotte plays her last verbal card and finds it taken up quietly by an inscrutable opponent; Maggie sees "in Charlotte's face, and felt it make between them, in the air, a chill that completed the coldness of their conscious perjury" (II, 258). Then she plants the "prodigious kiss" (II, 258), and like all first-class betrayers she betrays herself. From the moment of the kiss Charlotte must remain mute concerning her apprehensions of suspicion and dissatisfaction. She can catch no glimpse of where Maggie Verver is, or of where Maggie's omnipotent father may be; thus begins the tormenting imaginings and consequent paralysis which May Daniels has observed in Maeterlinck's plays. Charlotte becomes little more than a trapped, beautiful, stalking beast of the field. At the end of the chapter, when Charlotte reports that she and Adam will leave for America, Maggie understands that she "had done all."

Before the second important ritualistic embrace, that with her father, the great "Oriental deity in western dress,"[27] as Yeazell calls him, Maggie must have out with him the whole affair, and she does so in the novel's most complex unspoken conversation. It must be sufficiently explicit to prepare Adam to pack luggage, wife, and a mountain of art, and ship back to America. Yet it must be sufficiently quiet so that the fact of the adultery—or even the suspicion—never breaks the surface and demands verbal recognition. Words can get too far out of hand too rapidly, and Maggie will not risk the aftermath of such epiphanies. Therefore, she approaches her father with considerable trepidation:

> . . . if she were but different—oh, ever so different!—all this high decorum would hang by a hair. There reigned for her, absolutely, during these vertiginous moments, that fascination of the monstrous, that temptation of the horribly possible, which we so often trace by its breaking out suddenly, lest it should go further. . . . she might sound out their doom in a single sentence, a sentence easy to choose among several of the lurid. [II, 239–40]

In Chapter 37 Maggie says that so much has happened at her father's expense. "Say therefore I *have* had the feelings of a father. How have they made me a victim?" Adam Verver asks, and his daughter answers, "Because I sacrifice you." "But to what in the world?" At this point the richest silence of the book—and the most pivotal—stands between this father and daughter—and it takes up two full pages in the first edition. There are almost 800 words used to express the unspoken tension that passes between Adam's question and Maggie's universalized and near-meaningless answer. She merely chants the incremental rhythms of response—"Why I sacrifice you, simply, to everything and to everyone." There are many passages of this sort in *The Golden Bowl*, although none is as complex. Here the fully extended quotation is necessary.

"But to what in the world?"

At this it hung before her that she should have had as never yet the opportunity to say, and it held her for a minute as in a vise, her impression of his now, with his strained smile, which touched her to deepest depths, sounding her in his secret unrest. This was the moment, in the whole process of their mutual vigilance, in which it decidedly *most* hung by a hair that their thin wall might be pierced by the lightest wrong touch. It shook between them, this transparancy, with their very breath; it was an exquisite tissue, but stretched on a frame, and would give way the very next instant if either so much as breathed too hard. She held her breath, for she knew by his eyes, the light at the heart of which he couldn't blind, that he was, by his intention, making sure—sure whether or no her certainty was like his. The intensity of his dependence on it at that moment—this itself was what absolutely convinced her so that, as if perched up before him on her vertiginous point and in the very glare of his observation, she balanced for thirty seconds, she almost rocked: she might have been for the time, in all her conscious person, the very form of the equilibrium they were, in their different ways, equally trying to save. And they were saving it—yes, they were, or at least she was; that was still the workable issue, she could say, as she felt her dizziness drop. She held herself hard; the thing was to be done, once for all, by her acting, now, where she stood. So much was crowded into so short a space that she knew already she was keeping her head. She had kept it by the warning of his eyes; she shouldn't lose it again; she knew how and why, and if she had turned cold this was precisely what helped her. He had said to himself, "She'll break down and name Amerigo; she'll say it's to him she's sacrificing me; and it's by what they will give me—with so many other things too—that my suspicion will be clinched." He was watching her lips, spying for the symptoms of the sound; whereby these symptoms had only to fail and he would have got nothing that she didn't measure out to him as she gave it. She had presently in fact so recovered herself that she seemed to know she could more easily have made him name his wife than he have made her name her husband. It was there before her that if she should so much as force him just *not* consciously to avoid saying "Charlotte, Charlotte" he would have given himself away. But to be sure of this was enough for her, and she saw more clearly with each lapsing instant what they both were doing. He was doing what he had steadily been coming to; he was practically *offering* himself, pressing himself upon her, as a sacrifice—he had read his way so into her best possibility; and where had she already, for weeks and days past, planted her feet if not on her acceptance of the offer? Cold indeed, colder and colder she turned, as she felt herself suffer this close personal vision of his attitude still not to make her weaken. That was her very certitude, the intensity of his pressure; for if something dreadful hadn't happened there wouldn't, for either of them, be these dreadful things to do. She had meanwhile, as well, the immense advantage that *she* could have named Charlotte without exposing herself—as, for that matter, she was the next minute showing him.

"Why, I sacrifice you, simply, to everything and to every one." [II, 275–77]

Maggie comprehends her power "to say," but she does not say. Adam, on his side, sounds the depth of her silence; the metaphor suggests a word dropped deep and the wait for its return, with more account taken of the time it takes for the word to resurface than of the answered word itself. When Maggie finally responds, her reply is near tautology, but the charged encounter has changed the positions of the four players. Silence as an "exquisite tissue" becomes the tense membrane, a canvas "stretched on a frame," a blank surface which will *never* be painted upon by a young woman who has learned "something of the glitter of consciously possessing the constructive, the creative hand." The force of her action is unspoken as the two Ververs stand on opposite sides of a vivid chasm, perched above "unutterable" realities that await below.

The sense of *words* in the passage becomes insidious. Adam expects her to name Amerigo and thereby clinch his suspicions. He spies for the movement of Maggie's lips; she maintains her stillness. The syntax itself moves toward greater convolution than is usual in the late prose, but convolution is appropriate, for negation of expression becomes expression as ironies work themselves out—"it was there before her that if she should so much as force him *not* consciously to avoid saying 'Charlotte, Charlotte' he would give himself away." The troubling double negative suggests the difficulty of empowering forced silences with intention. Maggie holds her father off for a moment and then provides a structurally blank response, little more than a *stop* to their eloquent silence—the *words* take the place of the pause here: the reversal completes. Before Adam, under the extremity of pressure, breaks into perilous utterance, Maggie offers up her empty answer. Nothing of value has been said, but when Adam emerges from this scene he has the necessary understanding. "If you say much more we *will* ship" (II, 279), he responds—as if the words *said* were what he attended to as significant phenomena—"Why, you make me quite want to ship back myself. You make me quite feel as if American City would be the best place for us." For "us"? she asks. "For me and Charlotte," he responds.

The subsequent image presents Maggie's success.

> Ah, then it was that the cup of her conviction, full to the brim, overflowed at a touch! *There* was his idea. . . . he had named Charlotte, named her again, and she had *made* him— which was all she had needed more: it was as if she had held a blank letter to the fire and the writing had come larger than she had hoped. The recognition of it took her some seconds, but she might when she spoke have been folding these precious lines and restoring them to her pocket. [II, 279]

A blank letter held to the fire—impulses of silence, secret communication, and the need for infinite care all combine here—and the words she had planned for do appear, as if codes, in the midst of "sanctities of silence" (II, 279). Maggie "had drawn a long breath; she had made him do it *all* for her, and had lighted the way to it without his naming her husband. That silence had been as distinct as the sharp, the inevitable sound" (II, 280). Father as well as daughter experiences the communicative potential—"His very quietness was part of it now, as always, part of everything, of his success, his originality, his modesty, his exquisite public perversity, his inscrutable, incalculable energy" (II, 280).

After Maggie and Fanny joined in the wordless embrace which initiated their complicitous silence, Fanny spoke to her husband of Charlotte and Amerigo: "I can, I believe, keep them quiet." In the balcony scene Maggie then met Charlotte to exchange the portentous embrace which would silence her rival completely. Therefore Adam and his daughter meet on familiar ground to make their dramatic vow, a tribute to knowledge which characteristically must remain unspoken.

"I believe in you more than any one."

"Than any one at all?"

She hesitated for all it might mean; but there was—oh a thousand times!—no doubt of it. "Than anyone at all."

. . . "And that's the way, I think, you believe in me."

"Well then—?" She spoke as for the end and for other matters—for anything, everything, else there might be. They would never return to it.

"Well then—!" His hands came out, and while her own took them he drew her to his breast and held her. He held her hand and kept her long, and she let herself go; but it was an embrace that, august and almost stern, produced, for its intimacy, no revulsion and broke into no inconsequence of tears. [II, 282–83]

In his exhaustive phenomenological study of silence Dauenhauer establishes categories of "intervening silence," "fore-and-after silence," and "deep silence," and he shows how they share important characteristics:

(1) silence is an active human performance which always appears in connection with an utterance, (2) silence is never an act of unmitigated autonomy. Rather, (3) silence involves a yielding following upon an awareness of finitude and awe. The yielding involved in silence is peculiar inasmuch as (4) it is a yielding which binds and joins.[28]

"Deep silence" may best describe the condition of Milly Theale at the end of The Wings of the Dove; Dauenhauer's other categories describe the force of Maggie Verver as she draws everyone into deepening silence, allowing them autonomy on the one hand, but controlling them on the other, always yielding yet always binding. The explicit silences subsequent to the embraces—between Maggie and Fanny, between Maggie and Charlotte, between Maggie and Adam, and finally between Maggie and Amerigo—serve as potent examples of the "terminal silence which binds him who encounters it to interpret somehow the uncancellable gap between perception and discourse." Yet Dauenhauer goes further to elucidate the potential of silence for more profound communication where "the distinction between author and audience is sublated. There is no longer I-you. There is now we."

In their final tense scene Maggie and her father demonstrate the eloquent—and moving—"codiscourse" which Dauenhauer represents as one of the final stages of "bipolar discourse."

> There is a discernible cut between them, which I will call interpersonalizing silence. In the first shape, monologue, the author claims maximal control over the discourse and minimizes the audience's initiative. But even here the author cannot claim exhaustive control. On the basis of the recognition of other thematizing selves, who can thematize other things than he does or expects to do on his own, the author has to acknowledge the audience's initiative, however minimal it may be. Otherwise there is no monologue, only soliloquy. This same recognition of other thematizers also motivates the author to cut off his monologue. This cut, interpersonalizing silence, opens a space for another self to address the initial author.
>
> Interpersonalizing silence opens the way for dialogue, the second shape of discourse at this level. In this shape there is the permanent possibility of both a shifting of roles (the hearer becoming the author) and a blocking of some utterance (the audience leaves). This blocking is not of itself a cut of the sort in question here, for the audience may simply "turn the dial" to another speaker. The kind of cut at play here is also the penultimate foundation for the possibility of a shift from bipolar discourse, discourse in which the hearer is distinct from and in correlative opposition to the author, to the third level of interpersonal involvement in discourse, namely codiscourse.[29]

As the silent moment expands, Maggie allows the potential to shift from her to her father; yet the silence holds. By momentarily relinquishing control she transfers power to Adam, and through this intelligent, loving, trusting act of tense non-communication, they both are moved to understand the necessarily strong action which must be theirs. Dauenhauer speaks of the silent moment where there is "a yielding of autonomy for the sake of an interpersonal relationship which is more profound than that which can be established under the sway of autonomy,"[30] and such autonomy is what Maggie yields. In the scene where, suddenly aware of the limit of words to deal with critical issues, Maggie embraced Mrs. Assingham, they verged on despair. "Impossible," both women said, "yet the next minute [Maggie] had burst into tears over the impossibility, and a few seconds later, pressing, clinging, sobbing, had even caused them to flow, audibly, sympathetically, and perversely, from her friend" (II, 125). Finally, with her father, Maggie keeps control and lets herself out of his arms. No "inconsequence of tears," no "audible" tears follow. The scene's sadness comes of the ending which emphatically is recognized. After the embrace which, like priest and priestess, they carry out, both Ververs end on their feet.

Maggie Verver moves toward activity, but Charlotte and Amerigo find themselves increasingly restricted. After the encounter over the shattered golden bowl, Maggie and her husband parted with "extreme reserve"; since that moment there has been no reported discourse between the Prince and the Princess. Amerigo wanted to be left to his chill silence.

> "Leave me my reserve; don't question it—it's all I have, just now, don't you see?" . . . She had turned away from him with some such unspoken words as that in her ear, and indeed she *had* to represent to herself that she had spiritually heard them, had to listen to them still again, to explain her particular patience in face of his particular failure. [II, 226–27]

Just before the two Ververs depart for American City, Maggie reconsiders her husband, and she is said to have

> . . . recognised the virtual identity of his condition with that aspect of Charlotte's situation for which, early in the summer and in all the amplitude of a great residence, she had found, with so little seeking, the similitude of the locked cage. He struck her as caged, the man who couldn't now without an instant effect on her sensibility give an instinctive push to the door she had not completely closed behind her. . . . she had come to him in his more than monastic cell to offer him light or food. There was a difference none the less, between his captivity and Charlotte's—the difference, as it might be, of his lurking there by his own act and his own choice. [II, 346]

Like Charlotte, Amerigo is held by fear of what Maggie suspects, by "his fear of her fifty ideas," and she is moved by his pain to a "wish to repudiate or explain" (II, 347). She trembles for this victim of the silences she has fostered; momentarily she breaks down and attempts relief in words. She stands before Amerigo and holds a telegram from Charlotte. "With her eyes on him, doubling the telegram together as if it had been a precious thing and yet all the while holding her breath" (II, 347), she speaks of Charlotte and Adam "keeping the last night for each other." The statement presents extreme risks. With such a suggestive overture Amerigo might, even at this last moment, begin to explore what Maggie *knows*. She understands the risks—"She said these things as they came to her; she was unable to keep them back, even though, as she heard herself, she might have been throwing everything to the winds" (II, 349).

> She might have been losing her head verily in her husband's eyes—since he didn't know, all the while, that the sudden freedom of her words was but the diverted intensity of her disposition personally to seize him. He didn't know, either, that this was her manner—now she *was* with him—of beguiling audaciously the supremacy of suspense. [II, 349–50]

Here her weakness in the face of Amerigo's suffering moves her to risk losing her only tool for control.

If words at all, only meaningless words have passed between Maggie and Amerigo for months—"She, Maggie, had so shuffled away every link between consequence and cause, that the intention remained like some famous poetic lines in a dead language, subject to varieties of interpretation" (II, 353). Now both are moved to break the silence of separation and ambiguity and to collapse into the wordless embrace which, in this novel, repeatedly serves as the surest sign of understanding. Both falter into speech.

> "Ah, my dear, my dear, my dear—!" It was all he could say.
>
> She wasn't talking, however, at large. "You've kept up for so long a silence—!"
>
> "Yes, yes, I know what I've kept up. But will you do," he asked, "still one more thing for me?"
>
> It was as if, for an instant, with her new exposure, it had made her turn pale. "Is there even one thing left?"
>
> "Ah, my dear, my dear, my dear!"—it had pressed again in him the fine spring of the unspeakable. [II, 359]

At this point Maggie retreats to retain equipoise and control. The Prince asks her to "Wait" until after the other pair has departed. Then she might ask him the questions which she inevitably must ask. Maggie understands the danger of even such a minor break of the essential silence which she, and her stifled husband, long have kept.

> When she had drawn from him thus then, as she could feel, the thick breath of the definite—which was the intimate, the immediate, the familiar, as she hadn't had them for so long— she turned away again, she put her hand on the knob of the door. . . . There was something—she couldn't have told what; it was as if, shut in together they had come too far—too far from where they were; so that the mere act of her quitting him was like the attempt to recover the lost and gone. . . . That consciousness in fact had a pang, and she balanced, intensely, for the lingering moment, almost with a terror of her endless power of surrender. [II, 359–60]

Unnatural and nearly inhuman control emerges as the most secure means of dealing with the subtle terrors. Opposed to the impulses of the flesh and even the spirit, silence means nothing so much as control in *The Golden Bowl*.

So hard is her silent rule that Maggie stumbles into words and almost into a premature embrace. Amerigo stands before her—his face "only beautiful and strange—was bent upon her with the largeness with which objects loomed in dreams. She closed her eyes to it" (II, 361). Yet redemptive control develops as neither a passivity of luxurious oblivion, nor a closing of eyes, nor a seeing in dreams. It signifies neither abandonment nor renunciation. "Wait," she says; they both retreat, and her single utterance becomes "the word for both of them, all they had left, their plank now on the great sea" (II, 361).

Only after the ordeal of seeing off her father and his wife does Maggie accept the desired but somewhat annihilating embrace. The Prince returns to her; the fulfilling wordless gestures are presented in terms of sonoral positivity.

> It meant something for the Princess that her husband had thus got their son out of the way, not bringing him back to his mother; but everything now, as she vaguely moved about,

struck her as meaning so much that the unheard chorus swelled.
[II, 375]

The embrace finally comes, neither as retreat from pain nor as passive
denial; it provides ceremonial closure and also a beginning—"Yet *this*
above all—her just being there as she was and waiting for him to come
in, their freedom to be together there always—was the meaning most
disengaged" (II, 375–76).

Maggie recalls that between them still hangs the burden of explanation, the admission which she awaits and which the Prince expects
to deliver: "But what instantly rose, for her, between the act and her
acceptance was the sense that she must strike him as waiting for a
confession. This, in turn, charged her with a new horror: if *that* was
her proper payment she would go without money" (II, 377). She comprehends the ultimate irrelevance and impossibility of statement, and
she rejects any admission from her husband: "All she now knew, accord-
ingly, was that she should be ashamed to listen to the uttered word;
all, that is, but that she might dispose of it on the spot forever" (II,
377). Dauenhauer demonstrates the potential of silence to work for
delicate, unifying closure

> as a yielding which binds and joins. Intervening silence in its
> closing-opening function binds the already said to the pre-
> delineated sayable. Within an utterance, when a said word is
> closed off, an opening for the predelineated yet-to-be-said takes
> place. Fore-and-after silence binds the utterance into a unity.
> Perhaps the unity is fragile, but it is final. And deep silence
> binds him who performs it to that which is other and not
> inferior to him, however this other is interpreted.[31]

After the sufficiently charged wordless moment, for another instant
Maggie's fear rises, and then she provides the structurally empty utterance which does "dispose of all, on the spot, forever," and even that
utterance—irrelevant to the crisis the pair immediately comprehends—
may be read as another sign of silence. She dispenses with the unspeakable matter. With the genius of pattered small talk, evolved from a
"dead language," she eases them both back to the comfortably masking
social universe where words function to shroud reality: " 'Isn't she too
splendid?' she simply said, offering it to explain and finish." To finish.
She speaks these slightly mannered, now virtually absurd words about

part the dread must derive from Maggie Verver's awareness of how powerful she has been and how others have been bent under her benign but inexorable will. Stephen Spender spoke of the evil in *The Golden Bowl* as "simply the evil of the modern world,"[34] an evil which leaves no character untainted. I think what he meant has something to do with modern intelligence, with its extreme powers and extreme liabilities. The rarefied Jamesian personality attains a near-monstrous perceptual subtlety, and Maggie Verver's supremely intelligent wordlessness gives others gentle freedom to be bound by ruthless will. The relentless genius of the novel has been unspoken, and, at the end, Maggie Verver can face her husband only with relief and dread, as she shifts back again to puppet utterances, fully aware of the exquisite brutality which has transpired.

In the complex world of the twentieth century, words do fail to provide bridges for those who have learned their psychology, who have lost their traditions and gods and confidences, who have seen the center not holding, who beneath the shell of civilization have found foulness and putrefaction. Some writers who faced all this would work to abandon words and move toward absolute silence—they would simply write no more. Others, like James Joyce, would resist the views of men like Wittgenstein and make a new heaven and a new earth with words alone, but in the process abandoning a great deal that makes us human. By working with words, Henry James asserts the ability of man to communicate, to reach tense, imperfect understandings, to work human will to some extent with language. But he doubts, as some doubted before him and as many have doubted since, that language, and particularly speech, can adequately handle those tasks. In *The Golden Bowl* he offers a compromise. He presents, translated into words, the potential for dignity, for vitality, of a language of silence which might work to rejoin the pieces of a rapidly fragmenting world.

But the communicative compromise in *The Golden Bowl* offers little security. The silence in this book, as in *The Wings of the Dove*, provides a tenuous optimism, attainable only through magnificent intelligence and inhuman strain. The commonly held primacy of *logos* seems irrelevant indeed, especially in light of the shifting ground beneath the feet of these people. In discussing Beckett and Henry Miller, Ihab Hassan has said that

> literature has adopted a new attitude toward itself, and that silence is its metaphor—and if the metaphor dies, silence will

become the state toward which the entropy tends. The result
is anti-literature. The attitude this kind of literature expresses
is a judgement on ourselves in a time of outrage and apocalypse.[35]

Although neither Miller's explosive outbursts nor Beckett's evaporative
wanings resemble James's lush verbal landscape, signs of outrage, apocalypse, and the acrid waftings of *fin-de-siècle* decay slide through the
cracks into the gilded parlors. In 1921 Yeats and others would declaim
disjointure, but forces had been ranging loose below the surface long
before that. The movement in James is into a rich, fundamentally
conservative, late style which works—sometimes fearfully—to hold under
idiosyncratic linguistic pressure that which still might be held in an
ordered place. In discussing the Dadaist and Surrealist crises of language,
Hassan and Maurice Blanchot both speak of a varied literature moving
"toward its essence, which is disappearance," and finally entering "l'ère
sans parole," an epoch of wordlessness.[36]

When James wrote, however, the baroque temple of language stood
insecurely but still impressively, held in delicate equilibrium by pillars
of silence and pillars of talk. The issue is more profound than a complex
stylistic effort, for a philosophic leap attempts to reconcile an impure
eloquence with spreading recognition of the death of language and
perhaps other deaths. Prince and Princess, suddenly aware that the
living pulse of language is rapidly fading, meet at the end like primitive
beings abandoned on a barren new planet. Utterance, still perhaps
informed with some potential for beauty, hovers between them with
grotesque irrelevancy, neither more secure nor sacred than gold itself,
and surely no more able to evade the inevitabilities of mutability,
suffering, and isolation.

7 Conclusion: *Vita Activa*

"Gaze not too deeply into the abyss lest the abyss gaze back at you."
                                                                    Nietzsche

The modern age mistrusts the word, finding it increasingly unable to meet the imperatives of communication and understanding, as well as of the spirit. But the move into silence has been into darkness, now pulsing with promise, now with disaster, at the same time as ambiguously alive and dead as the ghosts in James's tales. Neither the silent preoccupations of *The Wings of the Dove* nor those of *The Golden Bowl* ring out strong or sure, and to some it will seem that both the *via negativa* and the *via positiva* come close to collapse. James's anxiety vibrates in an all-encompassing void which eventually must be called existential, one where consciousness drifts further and further out toward Pascal's infinite silent spaces and into isolation. Pascal, in William Barrett's view, "saw Nothingness as a possibility that lurked, so to speak, beneath our feet, a gulf and an abyss into which we might tumble at any moment. No other writer has expressed more powerfully than Pascal the radical contingency that lies at the heart of human existence—a contingency that may at any moment hurl us into non-being."[1] Yet James may have been as expressive of this contingency. From Roderick Hudson facing the alpine whiteness, to the universe of ghostly presences reclaiming their own vitality, to Milly Theale on the abyssal promontory, to Maggie Verver "vertiginous" before a breakdown so cosmic and atomic that it dismantles family, friendship, society, language, and communication itself, James's tense imagination weaves its carpet into increasingly evacuated chambers. His voice may not have had the singular clarity of Pascal's voice, but he was deeply aware of the intangible threat.

When E. M. Forster discovered the symmetries of Henry James, he wrote very well,[2] but he overlooked assertions against the crude possibilities of being and nothingness. What may sometimes seem adornment and decoration, clusters and balances of graceful shapes and attenuated movements, are nothing of the kind. The motives derive far more from terror than from ease. Like the pressure of silence in *The Golden Bowl*, working elusively to restrain the shatter into chaos, the recurring symmetries build links over alienating silent spaces. The Italians have a word for it, *sistemazione*, and it has little to do with the allure of a sunny land. Luigi Barzini, as fully aware as anyone of the darker motives behind the rareties of civilization, perceives the primitive fear beneath the shell of aristocratic harmonies.

> Fear can also be detected behind the Italian's peculiar passion for geometrical patterns, neat architectural design, symmetry in general, which is part of their love for show—mainly the fear of the uncontrollable and unpredictable hazards of life and nature; fear and also its shadow, a pathetic desire for reassurance. This compulsive predilection for regularity can be seen everywhere. It is only rarely utilitarian and seldom satisfies strictly functional needs, as almost always it is merely meant to please the eye and comfort the heart. Fruit and vegetable dealers spend precious minutes of the morning building fragile pyramids of their wares which they will have to demolish in the course of the day. The new maid will stubbornly remove every piece of furniture in your room from its accustomed place, every morning, to satisfy her ideal of symmetrical decorum. She will arrange the bibelots on the mantlepiece until it will look like the parody of an altar. Old gardens leave nothing to chance and unbridled nature. Their complicated patterns of hedges, gravel walks, fountains, statues, always strictly symmetrical, often puzzle the visitor, because they can only be fully admired by people flying over them in balloons, who see them as elaborate tapestries.[3]

The complicated pattern of hedges, gravel walks, syntax, digression, plot, structure, and void must puzzle and amaze the reader who would remain too close to the figured tapestry, for the surface and silences must be read for what they counter as much for what they clearly signify. Near the end of *The Golden Bowl* the Prince Amerigo tells his wife, "Everything, *cara*, is terrible in the heart of man," and their uneasy context edges out onto the Kierkegaardian landscape. The Prince's formulation seems the simplest yet most complex expression of an existential fear which develops in the increasingly silent atmosphere of the novels.

The Christian resolution, exercised with tingling fingertips in *The Wings of the Dove*, never takes hold, and the final novel reasserts a phenomenological universe, informed with extra-sensory perception but strangely devoid of spirituality. In much of the later fiction, even in the most elevated moments of *The Ambassadors*, no character manages the leap of faith a Kierkegaard finally attempted. When the Comtesse de Vionnet comes close to reasserting the early withdrawal of Claire de Cintré—out of the world and into some sort of cloistered retreat—a dark force, intense with formless anxiety, grips her. She faces Strether and comes up with "detestation," a general disgust fixed on ego and on existence itself.

> Oh but he wanted to hear. "Detestation of what?"
> "Of every thing—of life."
> "Ah that's too much," he laughed—"or too little!"
> "Too little, precisely"—she was eager. "What I hate is myself—when I think that one has to take so much, to be happy, out of the lives of others, and that one isn't happy even then. One does it to cheat one's self and to stop one's mouth—but that's only at best for a little. The wretched self is always there, always making one somehow a fresh anxiety. What it comes to is that it's not, that it's never, a happiness, any happiness at all, to *take*. The only safe thing is to give. It's what plays you least false." Interesting, touching, strikingly sincere as she let these things come from her, she yet puzzled and troubled him—so fine was the quaver of her quietness.[4]

Marie de Vionnet's final declaration may, to some, suggest movement toward the relief of *agape*, toward the otherworldly love that Milly Theale, with the help of New York attornies, almost delivers up. But this is probably not so. The woman Strether sees before him has pierced through veils of illusion and she shivers before isolation. Her wild denial of self looks more into darkness than toward the light, and it sounds with none of the confidence which might suggest salvation. Detestation of everything—at first too much, then too little. Sartre's later analysis would more pitilessly confront the irrelevancies of being and "the nausea of existence itself,"[5] but part of the quaver of quietness on Marie de Vionnet's lips already speaks of existential absurdity.

James's moral fiction attempts to present the force and modulations of social and psychological evil, but although the silences often get involved in the machinations of such evil, they more importantly function to establish a metaphoric atmosphere of fear, trembling, of amorphous identities, of likely impossibilities, and of an emptiness which sweeps negation beyond traditional moral discriminations. James's characters remain haunted by the pressure of non-being and non-expression, the recurrent "all-abysmal and all-unutterable"[6] of the notebooks and the novels, to such an extent that they often go static, and sometimes, as in "The Jolly Corner," annihilation of self crashes upon them. These preoccupations move thick and fast throughout, and all the talk of abysses and brinks sets these mostly Protestant souls on the edge of the great Void, at the forefront of what some have seen as the western world's long overdue encounter with Nothingness.

When the golden shell collapses, the diffuse and ambiguous center becomes a profound question. Speaking of the terror in the late fiction, Spender wrote "that the suffering of Henry James's over-perceptive characters, in particular the sleepless and choking nights of Maggie Verver, found expression in the physical suffering of the War. Maggie was, as it were, haunted by the ghosts of the future."[7] Spender reads James as a social novelist writing at a high and serious level, one whose tremors were stirred by prevision that the world would never again be the same, that the grand illusion would be gone for good and that blood would flow, that civilization's fiber would rip apart. James, however, was haunted by ghosts more amorphous and terrible than those of the First World War. The deep malaise of the West, deeper even than the wounds of battle or of holocaust, informs the sensibilities of the alienated characters who sit up rigid in splendid parlors or who sleep fitfully on canopied beds. In some way or another each passes the bounds of reason, communication, and positivity to emerge alone in a twilight world latent with anxiety, doubt, and sometimes apparent meaninglessness. Each for a time knows as consort some ambiguous silence. Whether like Roderick Hudson they collapse before it, or marry it as does Isabel Archer, or like Fleda Vetch finally romanticize it, whether like Milly Theale they confront it and find vitality in the ironic adventure of not stirring, or whether like Maggie Verver they use its threatening metaphor to manipulate others, the people in the fiction, splendidly surrounded by the material world, grow increasingly preoccupied with the antitheses of worldliness.

Silence becomes both the tool of conquest and the invincible adversary. Eventually Sartre would assert human freedom in the face of nullity—the creative negation of saying no. Throughout his career James also grapples with the ambiguity of the Void, one instant mysteriously fruitful, then suddenly barren; he refuses, however, to do what Sartre and others do—take its emptiness as the incontrovertible given. Above all as a profound ironist, he continually approaches the models of visionaries, like John of the Cross, who intuit rather than reason that the way down could be the way out, and that answers might derive only at the heart of chilling metaphors. Like Melville's whiteness of the whale—the whiteness of fulness, deity, intention, and order, or the whiteness of emptiness, atheism, and nihilism—James's silences lay pasteboard masks over existence's critical duality. Melville and James were alike in little, save perhaps for fundamental preoccupations. One could call silence the sound of metaphoric whiteness, so rich are they both in capacity for contrariety, for expressing both vitality and utter dessication.

The early impulses of the "théâtre du silence," and of Maeterlinck's "théâtre de l'attente," seeking fertility in restrained emotion and tightly delimited speech, were cautious when compared to such a dualistic struggle, one which Susan Sontag considered when she spoke of silence in terms of

> the unstable antithesis of "plenum" and "void." The sensuous, ecstatic, translinguistic apprehension of the plenum is notoriously fragile: in a terrible, almost instantaneous plunge it can collapse into the void of negative silence. With all its awareness and risk-taking (the hazards of spiritual nausea, even of madness), this advocacy of silence tends to be frenetic and overgeneralizing. It is also frequently apocalyptic and must endure the indignity of all apocalyptic thinking: namely, to prophesy the end, to see the day come, to outline it, and then to set a new date for the incineration of consciousness and the definitive pollution of language and exhaustion of the possibilities of art-discourse.[8]

Although Sontag echoes Sartre's "la nausée" and Pascal's plunge into the void, her remarks relate to the problems of James's major phase, a period of intense force but of troublesome diffusion and occasional aberration. "Frenetic" and "mad"—the consequence of preoccupation with silence does carry many of James's characters into an uneasy realm which, straining at the limits of classicism and tradition, looks toward expressionism and the surreal. The scattered fury of the governess of Bly, the perverse obsession of Maud-Evelyn's suitor, the hallucination of John Marcher, even the chilling exhilaration of Maggie Verver as she bends others to her will—the list is not difficult to draw out. "Overgeneralizing"—sickly but filled with gnomic expressiveness, Milly Theale confronts a mannerist painting and says she will "never be better than this," and Prince turns to Princess to tell her that everything in man's heart is terrible. The silences read as restraint, decorum, or over-refinement, instead of as focuses of emotionally, intellectually, and textually complex opposition, would deserve worse than the slight pejorative which Sontag suggests. At the same time opaque and rich, they provide characteristically luminous moments in the text.

Apocalypse, however, must show as a less palpable presence, for revelation in James flashes across no sea of fire. Yet there can be few more assured apocalyptic visions than Milly Theale's before the Bronzino, when after long silent contemplation of some ambiguous immensity, she offers up a syntactically scattered statement that renders anticlimactic and superfluous all which follows. The "indignity" of apocalypse—indignity perhaps because the sweep toward end and end's ambiguous silent perfection abandons this world as a debasement. Yet this world is the one to which Milly Theale must return, as must the many others, all after confrontations with a wordless force which knows none of the approximations and compromises of life. But Sontag justly deciphers apocalypse and not revelation, for while revelation wonderfully may sweep back the veils, apocalypse smells of blood and it tells of extreme crisis. As James violently strained for new linguistic expression, his mutely radiant late style moved away from unequivocal clarity, through ambiguities, into liturgical utterance, then into silence. Baroque and increasingly Catholic, it forcefully expresses the agonies of language and spirit, as well as the mortification of the flesh. It is perhaps for another study to question if the incomplete state of the novels James began after The Golden Bowl can in some way be attributed to the faltering sense of language which this study has discussed. Perhaps The Ivory Tower and The Sense of the Past might have provided surer resolution—silence more as Kierkegaardian plenum or as Sartrian void. As the opus stands completed, however, neither the transfiguration of

The Wings of the Dove nor the dissolution of *The Golden Bowl* seems certain.

Although a young Henry James spoke with condescension of Carlyle's dusty, smoky ejaculations, he stood in awe of the great man's "gospel of silence," finding it "never more rich than when he declared that things were immeasurable, unutterable."[9] Yet even then James felt uneasy, for he saw that eventually Carlyle's "imagination was haunted with theological and apocalyptic visions."

> One must allow, of course, for his extraordinary gift of expression, which set a premium on every sort of exaggeration; but even when one has done so, horror resides in every line of them. He is like a man hovering on the edge of insanity—hanging over a black gulf and wearing the reflection of its bottomless deeps in his face.[10]

The face could be John Marcher's, but many other faces throughout the fiction view the darkness, the brink, the bottomless deeps; and on many faces can be read signs of over-extension and near-madness. James understood the risks. The Carlylian fury of his novels is tempered by many forces—by symbolist aesthetic diffusion, by decadent irony, by mystical promises, and by an existential sympathy which finally, lastly, unites husband and wife. Emerson, James tells us, shared the views of his English friend Carlyle, but Emerson always answered extravagance with New England balance and restraint. He might have agreed with James's statement that "men live on the brink of mysteries and harmonies into which they never enter, and with their hands on the door latch, they die outside."[11]

In *Sartor Resartus* Carlyle wrote of the symbol's potential to provide "concealment and yet revelation: here therefore, by Silence and by Speech acting together, comes a double significance. And if both the Speech be itself high, and the Silence fit and noble, how expressive will their union be! . . . In the Symbol proper, what we call a Symbol, there is even, more or less distinctly and directly, some embodiment of revelation of the infinite."[12] James knew his Carlyle, as he knew his symbolists, but he went beyond the alluring yet loose formulations of the one and the sometimes strained, marionette utterances of the other. An artistically controlled silence is given sustained expression in his fiction. His characteristic late voice emerges as he confronts "the unutterable," not with vague romantic indulgence but with a complex sense of what Sartre called "the silent non-knowledge that the literary object has to communicate to the reader."[13] Frequently his vision—however luminous—becomes a dark vision and the darkness has little to do with the grim maneuvers of the salon. If Europe knows more, it actually seems to know not to hold the world so dear and not to believe at all securely in the promises of muscular, eager Protestantism. "La vielle sagesse" of a Marie de Vionnet is, in the end, mostly a weariness.

In 1896, in *The Treasure of the Humble*, Maeterlinck wrote of "the mysterious chant of the infinite, the ominous silence of the soul and of God, the murmur of Eternity on the horizon, the destiny or fatality that we are conscious within us, though by what tokens none can tell" but which deliver to all "le tragique quotidien." Must man, he asked, roar like the Atrides to get at life? Maeterlinck rejected the dagger-stroke revelation of conventional drama—even the rage of an Othello or of a Lear—and he asserted the belief that

> an old man seated in his armchair, waiting quietly under the lamplight, listening without knowing it to all the eternal laws which reign about his house, interpreting without understanding it all that there is in the silence of doors and windows, and in the little voice of the light, enduring the presence of his soul and of his destiny, bowing his head a little, without suspecting that all the powers of the earth intervene and stand on guard in the room like attentive servants, not knowing that the sun itself suspends above the abyss the little table on which he rests his elbow, and that there is not a star in the sky nor a force in the soul which is indifferent to the motion of a falling eyelid or a rising thought—I have come to believe that this motionless old man lives really a more profound, human, universal life than the lover who strangles his mistress, the captain who gains a victory, or the husband who "avenges his honor."[14]

This man could be Henry James himself, but surely he would never have voiced so unequivocally Maeterlinck's affirmation. James carried on the symbolist rebellion against exteriority, against a materialistic tradition, against rhetoric, but the payment the symbolists promised, and the security, never were his. Symons, Maeterlinck, Huysmans, Villiers de L'Isle Adam spoke of a shadowy passage where "description is banished that beautiful things may be evoked," where "the soul of things can be made visible," and "where literature, bound down by so many burdens, may at last attain liberty, and its authentic speech."[15] James never completely succumbed to the seduction of such appeals. Until the end of his career as a novelist he maintained the dialectical struggle, continually opposing the silent metaphors of plenum with those of void, always aware of the enriching potential of silences, but equally aware of their capacities to betray.

Twenty years after *The Renaissance* Pater's influence seems not to have been forgotten, and echoes of *La Gioconda* reverberate around Maeterlinck's old man. With Pater *La Gioconda*'s was "the head upon which 'all the ends of the world are come,' and her eyelids are a little weary."[16] Yet a change has taken place, for Leonardo's fantastic circle of rocks has transformed to an armchair, to a dimly lit room, and the central figure has become drier, more marginal, no longer a "diver in deep seas" but a lingerer over a tabled abyss. Maeterlinck's words sound like optimism, but the chill of the modern age seeps into even his most dramatic expression. More so for James himself did the symbolist's contemplative ideal become the constant and ineluctable question.

Hannah Arendt has traced with vigor, acuity, and depth of feeling the decline of such contemplation in our time. In *The Human Condition* she presents the difficulty of maintaining the integrity of what began to be lost in the seventeenth century, the *bio theoretikos* or the *vita contemplativa*, long held by various cultures as the only free way of life. Plato and Aristotle both believed that philosophy began with *thaumazein*, shocked wonder at the miracle of being, and that it ended in "the philosopher's experience of the eternal, which to Plato was *arrhēton* ('unspeakable'), and to Aristotle *aneu logou* ('without word'), and which was later conceptualized in the paradoxical *nunc stans* ('the standing now'),"[17] a condition perhaps correlative to Milly Theale's "adventure of not stirring." Arendt presents the fundamental hierarchy of human activity—of labor, of work, and then of action—and finally she demonstrates the debasement of modern man to the condition of *animal laborans*, one who has relinquished the reification of self-in-object that work provides, the disclosure of self directly which is action.

> If we compare the modern world with that of the past, the loss of human experience involved in this development is extraordinarily striking. It is not only and not even primarily contemplation which has become an entirely meaningless experience. Thought itself, when it became "reckoning with

consequence," became a function of the brain, with the result that electronic instruments are found to fulfill these functions much better than we ever could. Action was soon and still is almost exclusively understood in terms of making and fabricating, only that making, because of its worldliness and inherent indifference to life, was now regarded as but another form of laboring, a more complicated but not a more mysterious function of the life process. . . . The last stage of the laboring society, the society of jobholders, demands of its members a sheer automatic functioning, as though individual life had actually been submerged in the over-all life process of the species and the only active decision still required of the individual were to let go, so to speak, to abandon his individuality, the still individually sensed pain and trouble of living, and acquiesce in a dazed, "tranquilized," functional type of behavior. . . . It is quite conceivable that the modern age—which began with such an unprecedented and promising outburst of human activity—may end as the deadliest, most sterile passivity history has ever known.[18]

Arendt, in her attack on materialism's confusion of laboring, even of elegant, educated laboring, with action, writes without Maeterlinck's sentimentality; yet she comes to a similar end. Her argument indicates the vulnerability of both complex experience and thought in the modern *polis*—she finds no other human capacity so vulnerable as thought. To her only when the *vita activa* has essential reference in the *vita contemplativa*—which begins in the wonder of *thaumazein* and ends in the silence of *arrhēton*—"could life become active in its complete sense." Arendt finds the apparent activity of life as cunning and deceptive as James found it. She notes that after Cartesian doubt struck to the heart of man and led him to question if the world were real, much less immortal, "the only contents left were appetites and desires, the senseless urges of his body which he mistook for passion." Ultimately the Aristotelian orientation toward happiness is not central to Arendt's concern, and she dismisses much of what has been called happiness as a sterile "absence from pain" and little more than that.

The force of life for Arendt is fertility, and the test of life, for her as for James, is activity, a supremely subtle and complex function.

For if no other test but the experience of being active, no other measure but the extent of sheer activity were to be applied to the various activities within the *vita activa*, it might well be that thinking as such would surpass them all. Whoever has any experience in this matter will know how right Cato was when he said: *Numquam se plus agere quam nihil cum ageret, numquam minus solum esse quam cum solus esset*—"Never is he more active than when he does nothing, never is he less alone than when he is by himself."[19]

James seems to have had prevision of Arendt's view that an "existentially most important aspect, action, too, has become an experience for the privileged few, and those few who still know what it means to act may well be even fewer than the artists, their experience even rarer than the genuine experience of and love for the world." Henry James provides such experience, variously, brilliantly, but hesitantly evolved by a rare race who face wonder and then stillness, holding themselves back and thereby moving toward the *vita activa*, in an extreme effort to live human life among men.

Notes

PREFACE

1. Ihab Hassan, *The Dismemberment of Orpheus*, pp. 12–14.
2. Wayne Anderson, "The Rhetoric of Silence," p. 72.

CHAPTER 1: INTRODUCTION

1. Henry James, "The Correspondence of Carlyle and Emerson," p. 270.
2. Jean-Paul Sartre, "L'Homme Ligoté," p. 299.
3. Thomas Carlyle, *Sartor Resartus*, pp. 174–75.
4. Sartre, "L'Homme Ligoté," p. 299.
5. George Steiner, *Language and Silence*, pp. 12 ff.
6. F. O. Matthiessen, *Henry James: The Major Phase*, p. 25.
7. May Daniels, *The French Drama of the Unspoken*, p. 25. For the full text see Stéphane Mallarmé, "Crise de Vers," in *Divagations*. The English translation of this text is taken from T. G. West, *Symbolism*, pp. 1–12.
8. Henry James, *The Art of Fiction,"* in *The Portable Henry James*, pp. 387–88.
9. H. Peter Stowell, *Literary Impressionism: James and Chekhov*, p. 4.
10. Robert Goldwater, *Symbolism*, p. 1.
11. Arthur Symons, *The Symbolist Movement in Literature*, p. 7.
12. Goldwater, *Symbolism*, p. 26.
13. Symons, *Symbolist Movement*, pp. 153–54.
14. Daniels, *French Drama of the Unspoken*, pp. 5–6.
15. Maurice Maeterlinck, *The Plays of Maurice Maeterlinck*, I, 10.
16. Henry James, *The Wings of the Dove*, II, 335.

17. Discussed in Susan Sontag, "The Aesthetics of Silence," in *Styles of Radical Will*, p 10. See also John Cage, *Silence: Lectures and Writings*.

18. Sartre, "L'Homme Ligoté," p. 297.

19. Yasunari Kawabata, *Japan the Beautiful and Myself*, pp. 54–55.

20. Don Idhe, *Experimental Phenomenology: An Introduction*, p. 129.

21. Sontag, *Styles of Radical Will*, p. 10.

CHAPTER 2: THE PRELUDE TO SILENCE

1. Henry James, *The Ambassadors*, p. 29.

2. Henry James, *Roderick Hudson*, p. 276.

3. Henry James, *The Wings of the Dove*, II, 163.

4. Henry James, " 'Preface,' to *Roderick Hudson*," in *The Art of the Novel*, p. 18.

5. Ibid., p. 9.

6. Ibid., p. 3.

7. See in particular Kenneth Graham, *Henry James: The Drama of Fulfillment*, p. 37.

8. George C. Williamson, *Bryan's Dictionary*, V, 12.

9. Henry James, "The Metropolitan Museum's 1871 Purchase," in *The Painter's Eye*, p. 58.

10. Ibid., p. 56.

11. For a view which essentially disagrees with the evaluation made here, see Viola Hopkins Winner, *Henry James and the Visual Arts*, p. 106.

12. Henry James. *The American*, pp. 15–16.

13. Henry James, *The Golden Bowl*, II, 4–5.

14. Havelock Ellis, "Introduction" to J. K. Huysmans, *Against the Grain*, pp. 33–34.

15. Ibid., p. 14.

16. Daniels, *French Drama of the Unspoken*, p. 21. For fuller treatment see also "Supernaturalism and Naturalism" in Goldwater, *Symbolism*, pp. 148–77; see also pp. 1–50.

CHAPTER 3: THE SCENT OF DECADENCE

1. G. L. Van Roosbroeck, *The Legend of the Decadents*, p. 1.

2. Henry James, "The Death of the Lion" and "The Coxon Fund."

3. Malcolm Bradbury, "London 1890–1920," in *Modernism*, ed. Malcolm Bradbury and James McFarlane, p. 175.

4. H. Montgomery Hyde, *Henry James at Home*, p. 53.

5. Leon Edel, *Henry James: The Middle Years*, pp. 149–50.

6. Hyde, *Henry James at Home*, p. 53.

7. Max Beerbohm, "A Letter to the Editor," p. 284.

8. Arthur Symons, "The Decadent Movement in Literature," pp. 858–59.

9. J. K. Huysmans, *Against the Grain*, pp. 296–97.

10. Frank Moore Colby, "In Darkest James," p. 25.

11. Symons, "Decadent Movement," p. 859; Huysmans, *Against the Grain*, p. 297. English version in C. F. MacIntyre, trans., *French Symbolist Poetry*, p. 35.

12. Huysmans, *Against the Grain*, pp. 25–26. This comment is included in Havelock Ellis's lengthy introduction to the 1931 translation of *À Rebours*. Ellis provides an illuminating discussion of the interplay of decadent and Christian impulses, and he makes reference to Paul Bourget, who influenced James, as well as to Barès, Verlaine, and Mallarmé in particular.

13. Tzvetan Todorov, *The Poetics of Prose*, p. 143.

14. S. T. Coleridge, *Biographia Literaria*, II, 6.

15. Todorov, *Poetics of Prose*, p. 155.

16. Henry James, *The Portrait of a Lady*, p. 40.

17. Ibid., p. 508.

18. Martha Banta, *Henry James and the Occult: The Great Extension*, p. 131.

19. Henry James, "The Madonna of the Future," in *The Complete Tales of Henry James*, III, 47. Subsequent references to this uniform edition, which reprints "the original book form where there was one."

20. Carl Maves, *Sensuous Pessimism: Italy in the Work of Henry James*, p. 32. See also Darshan Singh Maini, *Henry James: The Indirect Vision*, p. 147.

21. *Literary Impressionism: James and Chekhov*, p. 5.

22. Ibid.

23. Todorov, *Poetics of Prose*, p. 177.

24. Ibid., p. 145.

25. John M. Munro, *The Decadent Poetry of the Eighteen-Nineties*, p. 5.

26. Yeats's typesetting presents Pater's prose with the look of poetry, with broken lines which begin, most often, with the conjunction "and." In his introductory remarks Yeats asks if Pater's description does not "foreshadow a poetry and a philosophy where the individual is nothing." W. B. Yeats, ed., *The Oxford Book of Modern Verse*, pp. xxx, 1. For the full prose text see Walter Pater, *The Renaissance*, p. 125.

27. James originally titled this story "The Way It Came," but later regretted the title and renamed it in subsequent editions. Edel's edition reprints the story under the original title, but most criticism refers to the tale with the renamed title—as is done here.

28. Dorothea Krook, *The Ordeal of Consciousness in Henry James*, p. 331.

29. Clive Scott, "Symbolism, Decadence, and Impressionism," in *Modernism*, ed. Bradbury and McFarlane, p. 208.

30. Ibid.

31. Ibid., p. 209.

32. Leon Edel, *Henry James: The Treacherous Years*, p. 326.

33. Philip M. Weinstein, *Henry James and the Requirements of the Imagination*, pp. 23–24, 53–54, 130–31.

34. Quentin Anderson, *The American Henry James*, p. 9.

35. Todorov, *Poetics of Prose*, p. 186.

36. Banta, *Henry James and the Occult*, p. 140.

37. Elizabeth Stevenson, *The Crooked Corridor*, p. 107.

38. John Keats, *The Letters of John Keats*, I, 387.

39. William Hazlitt, "On Shakespeare and Milton," *The Complete Works*, V, 47.

40. Symons, "Decadent Movement," p. 866.

41. Hannah Arendt, *The Human Condition*, p. 324.

CHAPTER 4: DIALECTICAL MARRIAGES

1. Henry James, *The Portrait of a Lady*, pp. 171–72.

2. J. K. Huysmans. *Against the Grain*, p. 78.

3. Ibid., p. 64.

4. Henry James, *The Portrait of a Lady* (New York: Scribner's, 1908), II, 16.

5. Quoted in G. M. Hyde, "The Poetry of the City," in Bradbury and McFarlane, eds., *Modernism*, p. 338.

6. Goldwater, *Symbolism*, p. 26.

7. Ibid.

8. Hyde, "Poetry of the City," p. 337.

9. *Portrait* (1908), II, 170.

10. Henry James, *Washington Square*, p. 8.

11. *Portrait* (1908), II, 246.

12. Susan Sontag, *Styles of Radical Will*, p. 20.

13. *Portrait* (1908), II, 176.

14. Daniels, *French Drama of the Unspoken*, p. 6.

15. Ibid., pp. 15–17.

16. Maurice Maeterlinck, *The Treasure of the Humble*, p. 22.

17. Ibid., p. 20.

18. Jules Huret, *Enquête sur l'évolution littéraire* (Paris: Charpentier, 1871), pp. 124–26. Quoted in Daniels, *French Drama of the Unspoken*, p. 53.

19. Richard Hovey, "Modern Symbolism and Maurice Maeterlinck," preface to Maeterlinck, *Plays*, p. 11. See also Daniels, *French Drama of the Unspoken*, p. 8.

20. George Steiner, *Language and Silence: Essays on Language, Literature, and the Inhuman*, p. 21.

21. Henry James, *The Notebooks of Henry James*, p. 35.

22. Weinstein, *Henry James and the Requirements of the Imagination*, p. 35.

23. Henry James, *The Wings of the Dove*, II, 163.

24. Joseph Conrad, "The Historian of Fine Consciences," in F. W. Dupee, ed., *The Question of Henry James*, pp. 45–46.

25. William H. Gass, "The High Brutality of Good Intentions," p. 67.

26. Goldwater, *Symbolism*, p. 1.

27. Graham, *Henry James: The Drama of Fulfillment*, pp. 132–33.

28. Henry James, *The Spoils of Poynton*, p. 295.

29. Sontag, *Styles of Radical Will*, pp. 4–5.

30. Flannery O'Connor, *The Habit of Being*, p. 226.

31. Henry James, "Mr. Tennyson's Drama."

32. Alfred Lord Tennyson, *Tennyson: Poems and Plays*, pp. 45–46.

CHAPTER 5: "VIA NEGATIVA"

1. Henry James, *The Wings of the Dove*, II, 356.
2. Leon Edel, *Henry James: The Master*, p. 116.
3. Ibid., p. 119.
4. Ibid.
5. G. K. Chesterton, *Orthodoxy*, p. 20.
6. Henry James, "Is There A Life After Death?" reprinted in F. O. Matthiessen, *The James Family*, pp. 602–14. Also see Richard A. Hocks, *Henry James and Pragmatistic Thought*, pp. 217–25.
7. "Is There A Life After Death?" p. 614.
8. Henry James, " 'Preface' to *The Wings of the Dove*," in *The Art of the Novel*, pp. 289–90.
9. Henry James, *The Spoils of Poynton*, pp. 302–3.
10. Henry James, " 'Preface' to *Wings*," p. 306.
11. Jean Pierrot, *The Decadent Imagination: 1880–1900*, p. 82. See also Pierrot's sections on "Mysticism," "Esthetic Roman Catholicism," and "Religious Unease."
12. Ibid., p. 81.
13. Ibid., p. 11.
14. Edel, *Henry James: The Middle Years*, pp. 149–50.
15. Paul Bourget, *Essais de Psychologie Contemporaine*; see also Pierrot, *Decadent Imagination*, pp. 12–16.
16. Pierrot, *Decadent Imagination*, p. 15; see Bourget, *Essais*, pp. 8–9.
17. Edel, *Henry James: The Middle Years*, p. 114.
18. Leon Edel, *Henry James: The Treacherous Years*, pp. 143–44.
19. Pierrot, *Decadent Imagination*, p. 83.
20. Ibid.
21. Ibid., p. 87.
22. Ibid.
23. Ibid.
24. Edel, *Henry James: The Master*, pp. 93–99.
25. William James, *The Varieties of Religious Experience*, p. 244.
26. Ibid., p. 246.
27. The letter is reprinted in Matthiessen, *The James Family*, p. 338.
28. William James, *Varieties of Religious Experience*, p. 397.
29. Max Beerbohm, "A Mote in the Middle Distance," in *A Christmas Garland*.
30. Symons, *Symbolist Movement*, p. 153.
31. Ibid., pp. 157–58.
32. Ibid., p. 165.
33. St. John of the Cross, *The Collected Works*, p. 149.
34. Ibid., p. 319.
35. Ibid., p. 320.
36. William James, *Varieties of Religious Experience*, p. 397.
37. For a discussion of the image of the dove, see particularly Eugene A. Maio, *St. John of the Cross: The Imagery of Eros*.

38. See Oscar Cargill, *The Novels of Henry James*, pp. 351–53.

39. Quoted in Jonathan Culler, *Structuralist Poetics*, p. 261.

40. Ibid., p. 260.

41. St. John of the Cross, *Works*, p. 638.

42. John of the Cross develops at least a dozen senses of the abyss in his poetry and prose. See particularly pp. 112, 160, 205, 224, 252, 270, 338, 493, 606, and 638. William James refers to the abyss as a central image for the mystical consciousness, and in his account of Ignatius Loyola, he cites and then discusses the following passage: "In one quarter of an hour I saw and knew more than if I had been many years together at the university. For I saw the Being of all things, the Byss and the Abyss, and the eternal generation of the Holy Trinity, the descent and the original of the world and of all creatures through divine wisdom" (*Varieties of Religious Experience*, p. 322).

43. Peter Brooks, *Melodramatic Imagination*, pp. 188–92.

44. There are other views of the dove metaphor. See in particular Ernest Sandeen, "*The Wings of the Dove* and *The Portrait of a Lady*: A Study of Henry James's Later Phase," 1060–75.

45. Edel, *Henry James: The Master*, p. 115.

46. Henry James, " 'Preface' to *The Wings of the Dove*," p. 306.

47. Culler, *Structuralist Poetics*, pp. 260–61.

48. Quoted in Daniels, *French Drama of the Unspoken*, p. 53. Also see Maeterlinck, "Preface" to *Théâtre*, vol. 1, p. iv.

49. William James, *Varieties of Religious Experience*, p. 330.

50. See *The Wings of the Dove*, I, 253, 259, 273; II, 113, 149, 156.

51. Sontag, *Styles of Radical Will*, pp. 14ff.

52. St. John of the Cross, *Works*, p. 716.

53. Goldwater, *Symbolism*, p. 31.

54. Henry James, *Washington Square*, p. 260.

CHAPTER 6: "VIA POSITIVA"

1. Steiner, *Language and Silence*, p. 12.

2. Ibid., p. 13.

3. Henry James, *The Golden Bowl*, II, 3–4.

4. T. S. Eliot, *Four Quartets*, in *The Complete Poems and Plays*, p. 121.

5. Maurice Maeterlinck, *The Treasure of the Humble*, p. 20.

6. Daniels, *French Drama of the Unspoken*, pp. 9–10.

7. Eliot, "Ash Wednesday," *Complete Poems and Plays*, p. 62.

8. Steiner, *Language and Silence*, p. 27.

9. See Daniels, *French Drama of the Unspoken*, pp. 60ff. Also, Maeterlinck, *La Princesse Maleine*, in *Théâtre*.

10. Ibid.

11. Maeterlinck, "Preface" to *Théâtre*, pp. i–ii. Discussed in Daniels, *French Drama*, p. 60.

12. Mario Praz, *The Romantic Agony*, p. 14.

13. Naomi Lebowitz, *The Imagination of Loving: Henry James's Legacy to the Novel*, p. 123.

14. Quoted in Bernard P. Dauenhauer, *Silence*, p. 18.

15. Dauenhauer, *Silence*, p. 18.

16. Richard Hovey, "Modern Symbolism and Maurice Maeterlinck," preface to Maeterlinck, *Plays*, p. 11.

17. Stephen Spender, *The Destructive Element*, p. 98.

18. Henry James, " 'Preface' to *Roderick Hudson*," in *The Art of the Novel*, ed. R. P. Blackmur (New York: Scribner's, 1934), pp. 16–17.

19. J. A. Ward, *The Search for Form*, p. 200.

20. Krook, *Ordeal of Consciousness*, p. 260.

21. Ibid., pp. 260, 262.

22. Ibid., p. 263.

23. Maves, *Sensuous Pessimism*, p. 136.

24. Sontag, *Styles of Radical Will*, p. 17.

25. Daniels, *French Drama*, p. 8.

26. Ruth Bernard Yeazell, *Language and Knowledge in the Late Novels of Henry James*, p. 109.

27. Ibid., p. 119.

28. Dauenhauer, *Silence*, p. 24.

29. Ibid., pp. 69–70.

30. Ibid., p. 71.

31. Ibid., p. 25.

32. Norman O. Brown, *Love's Body*, p. 259.

33. Sontag, *Styles of Radical Will*, p. 17.

34. Spender, *Destructive Element*, p. 96.

35. Ihab Hassan, *The Literature of Silence*, pp. 3–5.

36. Ibid.

CHAPTER 7: VITA ACTIVA

1. William Barrett, *Irrational Man*, p. 116.

2. E. M. Forster, *Aspects of the Novel*.

3. Luigi Barzini, *The Italians*, p. 117.

4. Henry James, *The Ambassadors*, p. 402.

5. See Barrett, *Irrational Man*, pp. 239–80.

6. Henry James, *Notebooks*, p. 321.

7. Spender, *Destructive Element*, p. 21.

8. Sontag, *Styles of Radical Will*, p. 32.

9. Henry James, "The Correspondence of Carlyle and Emerson," p. 270.

10. Ibid., p. 271.

11. Ibid.

12. Thomas Carlyle, *Sartor Resartus*, pp. 173–74.

13. Jean-Paul Sartre, "A Plea for Intellectuals," in *Between Existentialism and Marxism*, p. 272.

14. Maeterlinck, *Treasure of the Humble*, pp. 121–22. The passage, as quoted, follows the excerpted translation of Symons, *Symbolist Movement*, pp. 155–56.

15. Ibid., p. 9.

16. Walter Pater, *The Renaissance*, p. 125.

17. Arendt, *The Human Condition*, pp. 14, 15, 20.

18. Ibid., pp. 302–3, 309–10, 321–325.

Bibliography

Anderson, Quentin. *The American Henry James*. New Brunswick, N.J.: Rutgers University Press, 1957.

Anderson, Wayne. "The Rhetoric of Silence in the Discourse of Coleridge and Carlyle." *South Atlantic Review*, 49 (Jan. 84), 72–90.

Arendt, Hannah. *The Human Condition*. Chicago: University of Chicago Press, 1958.

Armstrong, Paul. *The Phenomenology of Henry James*. Chapel Hill: University of North Carolina Press, 1983.

Banta, Martha. *Henry James and the Occult: The Great Extension*. Bloomington: Indiana University Press, 1972.

Barrett, William. *Irrational Man: A Study in Existential Philosophy*. New York: Anchor, 1962.

Barzini, Luigi. *The Italians*. New York: Bantam, 1964.

Beerbohm, Max. "A Letter to the Editor," *The Yellow Book*, II, July 1894, pp. 281–84.

———. "A Mote in the Middle Distance," in *A Christmas Garland*. New York: E. P. Dutton, 1912.

Bourget, Paul. *Essais de Psychologie Contemporaine: Baudelaire—M. Renan—Flaubert—M. Taine—Stendhal*. Paris: A. Lemerre, 1883.

Bradbury, Malcolm, and James McFarlane, eds. *Modernism, 1890–1930*. Sussex: Harvester Press, 1978.

Bradbury, Nicola. *Henry James: The Later Novels*. Oxford: Oxford University Press, 1979.

Brennan, Gerald. *St. John of the Cross: His Life and Poetry*. Cambridge: Cambridge University Press, 1973.

Brooks, Peter. *Melodramatic Imagination: Balzac, Henry James, Melodrama and the Mode of Excess*. New Haven, Conn.: Yale University Press, 1976.

Brown, Norman O. *Love's Body*. New York: Random House, 1966.

Cage, John. *Silence: Lectures and Writings*. Middletown, Conn.: Wesleyan University Press, 1961.

Cargill, Oscar. *The Novels of Henry James*. New York: Macmillan, 1961.

Carlyle, Thomas. *Sartor Resartus*. London: Chapman and Hall, 1896.

Chatman, Seymour Benjamin. *The Late Style of Henry James*. New York: Barnes and Noble, 1972.

Chesterton, G. K. *Orthodoxy*. New York: Image Books, 1959.

Colby, Frank Moore. "In Darkest James," in *The Question of Henry James: A Collection of Critical Essays*, ed. F. W. Dupee. New York: Henry Holt & Company, 1945.

Coleridge, S. T. *Biographia Literaria; or Biographical Sketches of My Literary Life and Opinions*. Ed. J. Shawcross. Oxford: Oxford University Press, 1907.

Culler, Jonathan. *Structuralist Poetics: Structuralism, Linguistics, and the Study of Literature*. Ithaca, N.Y.: Cornell University Press, 1975.

Daniels, May. *The French Drama of the Unspoken*. Edinburgh: University Press, 1953.

Dauenhauer, Bernard P. *Silence: The Phenomenon and Its Ontological Significance*. Bloomington: Indiana University Press, 1980.

Dupee, F. W. *Henry James*. New York: William Sloane, 1951.

———. *The Question of Henry James: A Collection of Critical Essays*. New York: Henry Holt & Company, 1945.

Edel, Leon. *Henry James: The Untried Years: 1843–1870; The Conquest of London: 1870–1881; The Middle Years: 1882–1895; The Treacherous Years: 1895–1901; The Master: 1901–1916*. 5 vols. Philadelphia: Lippincott, 1953–1972.

Eliot, T. S. *The Complete Poems and Plays*. New York: Harcourt, Brace and World, 1962.

Forster, E. M. *Aspects of the Novel*. New York: Harcourt, Brace and World, 1927.

Gale, Robert L. *The Caught Image: Figurative Language in the Fiction of Henry James*. Chapel Hill: University of North Carolina Press, 1964.

Gass, William. "The High Brutality of Good Intentions." *Accent*, 18 (Winter 1958), 62–71.

Genette, Gerard. *Figures: Essais*. Paris: Editions du Seuil, 1966.

Goldwater, Robert. *Symbolism*. London: Allen Lane, 1979.

Graham, Kenneth. *Henry James: The Drama of Fulfillment: An Approach to the Novels*. Oxford: Clarendon Press, 1975.

Hassan, Ihab. *The Dismemberment of Orpheus: Toward a Postmodern Literature*. New York: Oxford University Press, 1971.

———. *The Literature of Silence: Henry Miller and Samuel Beckett*. New York: Knopf, 1967.

Hazlitt, William. *The Complete Works of William Hazlitt*. Ed. P. P. Howe. London: Dent, 1930.

Hocks, Richard A. *Henry James and Pragmatistic Thought: A Study of the Relationship between the Philosophy of William James and the Literary Art of Henry James*. Chapel Hill: University of North Carolina Press, 1974.

Hutchinson, Stuart. *Henry James, An American, As Modernist*. London: Vision Books, 1981.

Huysmans, J. K. *Against the Grain*. New York: Illustrated Editions, 1931. (No translator acknowledged.)

Hyde, H. Montgomery. *Henry James at Home*. New York: Farrar, Straus and Giroux, 1969.

Idhe, Don. *Experimental Phenomenology: An Introduction*. New York: G. P. Putnam's Sons, 1977.

James, Henry. *The Ambassadors*. New York: Harper and Brothers Publishers, 1903.

———. *The American*. Boston: James R. Osgood and Company, 1877.

———. *The Art of the Novel*. Ed. R. P. Blackmur. New York: Scribner's, 1934.

———. *The Complete Tales of Henry James*. Ed. Leon Edel. 12 vols. London: Rupert Hart-Davis, 1962–1964.

———. "The Coxon Fund," *The Yellow Book*, II, July 1894, pp. 290–360.

———. "The Correspondence of Carlyle and Emerson," *Century Magazine*, XXVI, July 1883, 384–95.

———. "The Death of the Lion," *The Yellow Book*, I, April 1894, pp. 7–52.

———. *The Future of the Novel: Essays on the Art of Fiction*. Ed. Leon Edel. New York: Viking, 1956.

———. *The Ghostly Tales of Henry James*. Ed. Leon Edel. New Brunswick, N.J.: Rutgers University Press, 1948.

———. *The Golden Bowl*. New York: Scribner's, 1904.

———. *Letters/Henry James*. Ed. Leon Edel. Cambridge, Mass.: Belknap Press of Harvard University Press, 1974.

———. "Mr. Tennyson's Drama." *The Galaxy*, September 1875, pp. 393–402.

———. *The Notebooks of Henry James*. Ed. F. O. Matthiessen and Kenneth B. Murdock. New York: Oxford University Press, 1971.

———. *The Painter's Eye: Notes on the Pictorial Arts*. Ed. John L. Sweeney. London: Rupert Hart-Davis, 1956.

———. *The Portable Henry James*. Ed. Morton Dauwen Zabel. Rev. ed. New York: Viking, 1968.

———. *The Portrait of a Lady*. Boston: Houghton, Mifflin and Company, 1881.

———. *Roderick Hudson*. Boston: James R. Osgood and Company, 1876.

———. *The Spoils of Poynton*. Boston: Houghton, Mifflin and Company, 1897.

———. *Washington Square*. New York: Harper and Brothers, 1881.

———. *The Wings of the Dove*. New York: Scribner's, 1902.

James, William. *The Varieties of Religious Experience*. Garden City, N.Y.: Image Books, 1978.

John of the Cross. *The Collected Works*. Trans. Kieran Kavanaugh and Otilio Rodrigues. Washington, D.C.: ICS Publications, 1979.

Kawabata, Yasunari. *Japan the Beautiful and Myself*. Tokyo: Kodansha International, 1969.

Keats, John. *The Letters of John Keats: 1814–1821*. Ed. Hyder Edward Rollins. Cambridge, Mass.: Harvard University Press, 1958.

Kimball, Jean. "The Abyss and *The Wings of the Dove*: The Image as Revelation." *Nineteenth-Century Fiction*, 10 (March 1956), 281–300.

Krook, Dorothea. *The Ordeal of Consciousness in Henry James*. Cambridge: Cambridge University Press, 1962.

Lebowitz, Naomi. *The Imagination of Loving: Henry James's Legacy to the Novel*. Detroit: Wayne State University Press, 1965.

MacIntyre, C. F., trans. *French Symbolist Poetry*. Berkeley: University of California Press, 1958.

Maeterlinck, Maurice. *The Plays of Maurice Maeterlinck*. 2 vols. Trans. Richard Hovey. Chicago: Stone and Kimball, 1894.

———. *Théâtre*. Brussels: Lacomblez, 1911.

———. *The Treasure of the Humble*. Trans. Alfred Sutro. New York: Dodd, Mead, 1897.

Maini, Darshan Singh. *Henry James: The Indirect Vision: Studies in Themes and Techniques*. Bombay and New Delhi: McGraw Hill, 1973.

Maio, Eugene A. *St. John of the Cross: The Imagery of Eros*. Madrid: Playor, 1973.

Mallarmé, Stéphane. *Divagations*. Paris: Fasquelle, 1897.

Marks, Sita Patricia. "The Sound and the Silence: Nonverbal Patterns in *The Wings of the Dove*." *Arizona Quarterly*, 27 (Summer 1971), 143–50.

Matthiessen, F. O. *Henry James: The Major Phase*. New York: Oxford University Press, 1944.

———. ed. *The James Family, Including Selections from the Writings of Henry James, Senior, William, Henry, and Alice James*. New York: A. A. Knopf, 1947.

Maves, Carl. *Sensuous Pessimism: Italy in the Work of Henry James*. Bloomington: Indiana University Press, 1973.

Merleau-Ponty, Maurice. *Signs*. Trans. Richard C. McCeay. Evanston, Ill.: Northwestern University Press, 1964.

Munro, John M. *The Decadent Poetry of the Eighteen-Nineties*. Beirut: American University of Beirut, 1970.

O'Connor, Flannery. *The Habit of Being: Letters*. New York: Farrar, Straus and Giroux, 1979.

Pater, Walter. *The Renaissance: Studies in Art and Poetry*. London: Macmillan, 1910.

Perosa, Sergio. *Henry James and the Experimental Novel*. Charlottesville: University Press of Virginia, 1978.

Pierrot, Jean. *The Decadent Imagination: 1880–1900*. Trans. Derek Coltman. Chicago: University of Chicago Press, 1981.

Praz, Mario. *The Romantic Agony*. 2d ed. Trans. Angus Davidson. London: Oxford University Press, 1951.

Rowe, John Carlos. *Theoretical Dimensions of Henry James*. Madison: University of Wisconsin Press, 1985.

Sandeen, Ernest. "*The Wings of the Dove* and *The Portrait of a Lady*: A Study of Henry James's Later Phase," *PMLA*, 69 (Dec. 1954), 1060–75.

Sartre, Jean-Paul. *Between Existentialism and Marxism*. Trans. John Matthews. London: NLB, 1974.

———. *Situations I*. Paris: Gallimard, 1947.

Sears, Sallie. *The Negative Imagination: Form and Perspective in the Novels of Henry James*. Ithaca, N.Y.: Cornell University Press, 1968.

Sontag, Susan. *Styles of Radical Will*. New York: Farrar, Straus, and Giroux, 1961.

Spender, Stephen. *The Destructive Element: A Study of Modern Writers and Beliefs*. Philadelphia: Albert Saifer, 1953.

Steiner, George. *Language and Silence: Essays on Language, Literature, and the Inhuman*. New York: Atheneum, 1967.

Stevenson, Elizabeth. *The Crooked Corridor: A Study of Henry James*. New York: Macmillan, 1949.

Stowell, H. Peter. *Literary Impressionism: James and Chekhov*. Athens: University of Georgia Press, 1980.

Symons, Arthur. "The Decadent Movement in Literature," *Harpers*, 87, November 1893, pp. 858–67.

———. *The Symbolist Movement in Literature*. London: William Heinemann, 1899.

Tennyson, Alfred Lord. *Tennyson: Poems and Plays*. Ed. T. Herbert Warren. London: Oxford University Press, 1965.

Todorov, Tzvetan. *The Poetics of Prose*. Ithaca, N.Y.: Cornell University Press, 1977.

Van Roosbroeck, G. L. *The Legend of the Decadents*. New York: Columbia University Press, 1927.

Wagenknecht, Edward. *Eve and Henry James: Portraits of Women and Girls in His Fiction*. Norman: University of Oklahoma Press, 1978.

Ward, J. A. *The Search for Form: Studies in the Structure of James's Fiction*. Chapel Hill: University of North Carolina Press, 1967.

Weinstein, Philip M. *Henry James and the Requirements of the Imagination*. Cambridge, Mass.: Harvard University Press, 1971.

West, T. G., ed. and trans. *Symbolism: An Anthology*. London: Methuen, 1980.

White, Allon. *The Uses of Obscurity: The Fiction of Early Modernism*. London: Routledge and Kegan Paul, 1981.

Williamson, George C. *Bryan's Dictionary of Painters and Engravers*. New York: Macmillan, 1905.

Winner, Viola Hopkins. *Henry James and the Visual Arts*. Charlottesville: University of Virginia Press, 1970.

Yeats, W. B., ed. *The Oxford Book of Modern Verse*. New York: Oxford University Press, 1936.

Yeazell, Ruth Bernard. *Language and Knowledge in the Late Novels of Henry James*. Chicago: University of Chicago Press, 1976.

Index